French Dishes For American Tables

Over 500 Traditional Recipes

By

Pierre Caron

# CHAPTER I.
## *SOUPS.*

1. **Consommé, or Stock.** Put in a stock-pot a roast fowl (or the carcass and remains of a fowl), a knuckle of veal, three pounds of beef, and three quarts of water. When the scum begins to rise, skim carefully until it quite ceases to appear. Then add a carrot, a turnip, an onion, a leek, two cloves, a little celery, and a little salt. Simmer very gently four hours. Remove every particle of grease, and strain through a flannel kept for the purpose. This soup is the foundation of most soups and sauces. To clarify: when necessary that the soup should be very clear, clarify it in the following manner: Put in a saucepan a pound of chopped raw beef (off the round is preferable), which mix with an egg and two glasses of water, and pour into your consommé. Simmer very gently for an hour, and strain.

2. **Bouillon, or Beef Broth.** Put into a stock-pot three pounds of a shin of beef, one pound of a knuckle of veal, and three quarts of water, and simmer gently. As soon as the scum begins to rise, skim carefully until it quite ceases to appear. Then add salt, two carrots, the same of onions, leeks, turnips, and a little celery. Simmer gently four hours, strain, and serve.

3. **Bouillon Maigre.** Take six medium-sized carrots, as many turnips, a bunch of celery, and two leeks. Boil them in water for a few moments, drain, put them in cold water for a moment, after which put them into three quarts of water, adding two cloves, and boil gently three hours. Add a little salt, put through a sieve, heat again on the fire, and serve.

4. **BouillonMaigr eofFish.** Put into three quarts of water two pounds of black bass, two pounds of pike, and one pound of eels. Add to these two onions, two carrots, one head of celery, two cloves, and a little salt. Simmer gently for two hours, and strain. This bouillon is used as a foundation for all soups and sauces composed of fish.

5. **Pot-au-Feu.** Put into a saucepan three quarts of water, two pounds of beef cut in slices, a fowl partially roasted, a knuckle of veal, and a little salt.

Simmer gently, and as soon as boiling begins, skim carefully. Add two carrots, two turnips, two leeks, a few branches of celery, an onion stuck with two cloves, and boil four hours. Drain your vegetables carefully, remove every particle of grease from your soup, strain, pour it over your vegetables, and serve.

6. **Soup à la Julienne** (Vegetable Soup). Divide two medium-sized carrots in two, then cut into very thin slices of about an inch long; take the same quantity of turnips, leeks, onions, and a few pieces of celery, all cut into thin slices, and put them into a saucepan, with a piece of good butter, on a gentle fire, stir softly until the vegetables begin to color slightly, add three pints of consommé (or stock, Art. 1), and boil gently one hour. Ten minutes before serving put in three or four leaves of lettuce, the same of sorrel, and a little chervil chopped up, boil a little longer, adding a pinch of sugar, and a tablespoonful of green peas previously boiled.

7. **Soup à la Printanière.** This soup is made exactly as the foregoing, except with the addition of asparagus-tops to the other vegetables, which, instead of being in slices, are cut out in fancy shapes with a vegetable-cutter, which may be procured at any hardware-shop.

8. **Soup à la Brunoise.** Cut into square pieces, as small as possible, a carrot, a turnip, an onion, a leek, and a few pieces of celery. Stew gently in a saucepan with a little butter, stir softly until beginning to color lightly, drain, and put into three pints of consommé (see Art. 1), which boil gently for an hour, skim off the grease carefully, and serve.

9. **Soup à la Paysanne.** Take two tablespoonfuls of white beans, the same of green peas. Cut in slices a carrot, a little celery, a turnip, a leek, a cucumber, and a few string-beans; add a dozen little onions and a pinch of sugar. Put these into three pints of consommé (or stock), which boil gently an hour. Before serving you may add a few pieces of bread cut in small squares and fried in butter.

10. **Soup with (farcied) Lettuce.** Boil ten moderate-sized lettuce, then dip them in cold water, drain and press the water from them. Separate them in two, season with a little pepper and salt, then lay a tablespoonful of farce on the half of one lettuce, and cover with the other half. Wrap up each lettuce with a piece of *very thin* larding pork, place them carefully in a

saucepan containing half a pint of consommé (or stock, Art. 1), and a few branches of parsley, inclosing a clove of garlic, three pepper-corns, three cloves, and tie all together. After boiling gently an hour, drain the lettuce, remove the larding pork, the parsley, and its seasoning. Have boiling three pints of consommé (Art. 1), into which place your lettuce, and serve. It would be well to tie the larding pork around the lettuce, so that the farce should not escape.

11. **Farce.** Place in a saucepan four ounces of very fresh bread-crumbs and a cup of consommé (or stock, Art. 1). Simmer gently for ten minutes, at the end of which time stir constantly with a wooden spoon, and boil for ten minutes longer, so as to form a soft paste. This done, put it on a plate to cool. Take four ounces of the breast of a chicken, from which remove the skin and sinews, and pound extremely fine. Add to this your bread-crumbs, in quantity about three quarters as much as you have of chicken, and pound together until well mixed; season with a little salt and white pepper, a very little nutmeg, and a piece of butter. Then pound again, adding by degrees two eggs, until you have obtained a fine, smooth paste. This mixture is used for all farces of chicken. Veal, fish, and game are treated in the same manner. Quenelles are also made of this mixture, by forming it into small balls, and poaching them in boiling water for two minutes.

12. **Sorrel Soup** (clear). Wash a good handful of sorrel, which chop up together with a lettuce and a teaspoonful of chopped chervil, and put in a saucepan with half an ounce of butter. When beginning to color lightly, add three pints of consommé (or stock, Art. 1), and boil gently twenty minutes. Add a pinch of sugar, and skim the grease carefully from your soup. Serve with small squares of bread fried in butter a light brown.

13. **Cucumber Soup with Green Peas.** Cut two cucumbers in small pieces, and, adding a pinch of sugar, cook in a little stock for about half an hour, then add a pint of green peas, previously boiled, and serve in three pints of consommé (or stock, Art. 1).

14. **Soup à la Pluche de Cerfeuil** (Chervil Soup). Fry in butter pieces of bread cut in small squares, after which drain them. Pick and clean a handful of chervil, and, taking only the ends of the leaves, serve, together with bread, in three pints of consommé.

15. **Potage aux Pointes d'Asperges** (Asparagus Soup). Take from two bunches of asparagus only the small green ends, wash them, and then put them in a saucepan in boiling water with a little salt, and a very little soda, so as to make them very green. Then, having thoroughly boiled them, put them for a moment in cold water, drain, and serve them in three pints of consommé (Art. 1), and add small squares of bread fried in butter.

16. **Croûtes au Pot.** Cut a carrot, a turnip, and a few pieces of celery in small pieces, blanch them in hot water, drain them, and boil with three pints of consommé (or stock, Art. 1); take four French rolls, which divide in two, taking out all the soft part, and butter the inside. Put them in the oven, and, as soon as they become browned, serve them in your consommé, with the addition of a tablespoonful of green peas previously boiled.

17. **Consommé with Poached Eggs.** Put in a saucepan with some boiling water a tablespoonful of vinegar and a pinch of salt, in which poach eight eggs. Then take them out and put them in cold water, so as to pare the whites perfectly round, lay them again in hot water for a moment, and serve in three pints consommé (Art. 1).

18. **Consommé Royal.** Break into a bowl two eggs, with which mix thoroughly half a glass of milk. Butter a little saucepan, into which strain your eggs and milk. Then put your saucepan into a flat pan, which you have half filled with boiling water, and place in a moderate oven for about thirty minutes. Take it out to cool, and when cold, cut in little squares, and serve in three pints of consommé (see Art. 1). If desired, add a handful of green peas, a few thin slices of carrots, a few string-beans cut in diamond-shapes, or a few green ends of asparagus, all previously boiled.

19. **Soup à la Princesse.** Boil a fowl in a little stock for two hours. Take it out and let it become cold. Boil two tablespoonfuls of barley, which afterward put in cold water for a moment. Also boil about a handful of green peas. Cut the chicken into small pieces, after having carefully removed all skin, and put into three pints of consommé (see Art. 1 ), together with the barley and peas, boil for five minutes and serve.

20. **Beef Soup.** Boil two ounces of barley with a little salt for ten minutes, then put in cold water for a moment, cut into small squares four ounces of cold beef, which, with the barley, and about an eighth of a can of

tomatoes, boil for ten minutes in three pints of consommé (or stock, Art. 1), and serve.

21. **Vermicelli Soup.** Take four ounces of vermicelli, which boil in hot water for twenty minutes, then put in cold water for a moment and drain. Put three pints of consommé (Art. 1) in a saucepan, and, as soon as it begins to boil, pour in the vermicelli; boil for ten minutes, and serve.

22. **Vermicelli Soup with Green Peas.** Prepare as the foregoing, and just before serving add eight tablespoonfuls of green peas previously boiled.

23. **FarinaSoup.** Add to three pints of boiling consommé (or stock, Art. 1) two ounces of farina by degrees, stirring constantly with a wooden spoon, so as to prevent thickening into lumps, and, after boiling gently twenty minutes, serve.

24. **Arrowroot Soup.** Put in a saucepan four teaspoonfuls of arrowroot, which moisten with a little cold stock, so as to form a smooth paste; then add to it three pints of hot stock, taking care to stir with a spoon from time to time, so as not to stick to the saucepan, and, after boiling gently twenty minutes, serve.

25. **Soup with Italian Paste.** Take four ounces of Italian paste and blanch in boiling water with a little salt for twenty minutes. Drain, and put in three pints of consommé (see Art. 1), boil for ten minutes, and serve.

26. **Sago Soup.** Take two ounces of sago, which boil gently in three pints of consommé (see Art. 1) for thirty minutes, taking care to stir constantly with a spoon; serve.

27. **Tapioca Soup.** Put in three pints of consommé (Art. 1) four ounces of tapioca, which stir constantly; boil for forty minutes, and serve.

28. **Potage de Nouilles** (Noodle Soup). Take four ounces of flour, very little salt, and two yolks of eggs, with which make a tolerably firm paste. Roll it out very thin, taking care to sprinkle some flour on the table, so that the paste does not stick. Fold it in two; cut it in very thin slices of about an inch long, and blanch them in boiling water ten minutes; after which put in cold water for a moment, drain, and serve in three pints of boiling consommé (see Art. 1).

29. **Soup with Rice.** Take four ounces of rice, which wash well, then boil for ten minutes, and put in cold water for a moment. Boil the rice in three pints of consommé (see Art. 1) for forty minutes; skim and serve.

30. **Rice Soup à la Créole.** Take six ounces of rice, which prepare as the foregoing, and ten minutes before serving add about an eighth of a can of tomatoes, and a little cayenne pepper; boil for a moment, and serve.

31. **Chicken Consommé.** Take a chicken, cut it in pieces and put in a saucepan with two quarts of water, and let it simmer gently until the scum begins to rise, skim until every particle is removed; then add salt, a carrot, an onion, a turnip, and a little celery. Boil gently for two hours, strain, and serve.

32. **Chicken Giblet.** Cut a chicken, an onion, and a little ham, each in small pieces. Put all together, in a saucepan, on the fire, and add half an ounce of butter. When beginning to color slightly, add three points of consommé (see Art. 1), and a pinch of rice; and, after boiling three quarters of an hour, add two tablespoonfuls of tomatoes, boil five minutes longer, and serve.

33. **Chicken Gumbo.** Cut in very small squares one ounce of raw ham and an onion, which put in a saucepan, with a piece of butter, and the wings of a chicken cut in small pieces. When beginning to color slightly, add three pints of consommé (or stock, Art. 1) and a pinch of barley. Boil an hour. Half an hour before serving, put in ten okra-pods cut in slices, five tablespoonfuls of tomatoes, and a little red pepper.

34. **Chicken Okra, with Oysters.** Prepare as the foregoing, without the barley. Blanch two dozen oysters, which drain, and add to your soup just before serving.

35. **English Mutton Broth.** Take half a pound of cold mutton and an onion, cut each in very small pieces, and put in a saucepan with half an ounce of butter. When beginning to color slightly, add three pints of consommé (or stock, Art. 1), a carrot, and a turnip, cut in small even pieces. Boil an hour, skim off the grease, and just before serving add two ounces of barley previously boiled.

36. **Mullagatawny Soup.** Cut into small pieces an onion, a carrot, a few pieces of celery, and a slice of ham, which put in a saucepan on a moderate fire, with half an ounce of butter, until they begin to color slightly. Add one quart of consommé (or stock, Art. 1) and boil for an hour; add a pinch of curry, a little mullagatawny paste, which moisten with a little cold stock, and, after adding a pint of stock, boil for five minutes, and serve. Cold mutton, veal, or chicken, cut in small pieces, may be added to this if desired.

37. **French Ox-tail Soup.** Cut an ox-tail in small pieces, also an onion, and put in a saucepan with a little butter. When they begin to color slightly, add three pints of consommé (or stock) and boil gently for two hours. Skim off the grease, add one ounce of barley which you have previously boiled, and about an eighth of a can of tomatoes; boil ten minutes, and serve.

38. **English Ox-tail Soup.** Proceed as for the foregoing, except instead of consommé add three pints of Spanish sauce (see Art. 80), with very little thickening. Boil for two hours, and add a little barley, a little salt, a carrot, previously boiled and cut in slices, and four tablespoonfuls of tomatoes. Twenty minutes before serving add a good glass of sherry, boil for a moment, and serve.

39. **Mock-Turtle Soup.** Take a scalded calf's head, boil it in hot water for twenty minutes, drain, and put it in cold water. Then place it in a saucepan with three quarts of water, a carrot, an onion, four cloves, three cloves of garlic, a few branches of parsley, a tablespoonful of vinegar, and a little salt. Mix well three tablespoonfuls of flour in a little water, which add to the other ingredients and boil gently for an hour and a half. Drain, and when cold cut the calf's head into small pieces. Then add three pints Spanish sauce (see Art. 80), boil gently twenty minutes, and, just before serving, also add one good glass of sherry, a little red pepper, and two hard-boiled eggs chopped up, the yolks and whites separately, and the peel of a lemon cut in small pieces.

40. **Calf's-feet Soup.** Blanch two calf's feet for ten minutes, then put them in cold water for a moment. Afterward place them in a saucepan, with an onion, a carrot, a pinch of thyme, a bay-leaf, a clove of garlic, a little parsley, the juice of a lemon, and a little salt. Boil about an hour, or until

very tender, and let them cool. Then cut the calf's feet in small pieces, which put in three pints of boiling consommé (or stock), with the addition of two wineglasses of sherry, and serve.

41. **American Green-Turtle Soup.** Take a turtle, and let it bleed for six hours, taking care that the head hangs downward. Then divide the two shells, pressing your knife on the lower one so as not to disturb the intestines, which take entire and throw immediately away. Detach the fins and fleshy parts, putting aside any not needed for the soup, and which may be put to use afterward in an entrée, or broiled. After having cleaned them put them in a saucepan, with a sufficient quantity of water to cover them. Boil them, taking care to see from time to time that the shells of the fins detach themselves. Put them in cold water for a moment, drain, and cut them in small pieces, which place in a saucepan, with three pints of consommé (or stock, [Art. 1](#)). Boil gently for three hours, add four glasses of sherry and some Spanish sauce (see [Art. 80](#)). Boil hard four eggs, pound the yolks, adding a little salt and pepper, and the yolk of a raw egg. Form this mixture into little balls, putting a little flour on your hands to roll them. Poach them in boiling water, throw them into your soup, and, after boiling an instant, serve.

42. **Green-Turtle Soup à la Londonderry.** Proceed as for the foregoing, but instead of Spanish sauce add three pints of consommé (or stock, [Art. 1](#)) and a glass of sherry. Boil gently half an hour, and serve.

43. **Terrapin Soup.** Take a live terrapin, and, removing the claws, soak in boiling water for about three minutes. With a cloth remove the shells, and, proceeding as for the green turtle, cut it in small pieces and boil it in consommé (stock, [Art. 1](#)). When the terrapin is cooked, add some Spanish sauce ([Art. 80](#)), with two glasses of sherry, boil gently for twenty minutes, make some little balls prepared in the manner described in green-turtle soup ([Art. 41](#)), and serve in your soup.

44. **Soup à la d'Orsay.** Wash the ends of a bunch of asparagus, which boil with a little salt and a very little soda, drain them and put them into cold water. Press them through a sieve, add two yolks of raw eggs and three pints of consommé (stock), and, when boiling, a pinch of sugar and an ounce of butter. Take the breasts of two roast pigeons, then add to your soup

when serving, and eight small eggs, which boil soft (but sufficiently hard to remove the shells), and serve in your soup.

45. **Soup aux Quenelles de Volaille.** Prepare some quenelles (see Art. 11) and serve them in three pints of consommé (Art. 1).

46. **Consommé Rachel.** Spread on a sheet of tin half a pound of farce (Art. 11) of chicken (Art. 11) and put in the oven for three or four minutes. Put it aside to cool, and then with a cutter for the purpose form into round flat shapes. Place in a saucepan four ounces of flour, which mix in three pints of cold consommé (Art. 1), boil gently for half an hour, stirring with a spoon from time to time, so that it does not stick to the saucepan. Strain, remove from the fire, and add three yolks of eggs which you have mixed in a little water, a tablespoonful of green peas previously boiled, the small rounds of chicken farce, and serve.

47. **Rye Soup à l'Allemande.** Wash well half a pound of rye, and add three pints of consommé (stock, Art. 1), a few pieces of celery, three leeks, a little salt and pepper, and boil gently three hours. Remove the leeks and celery, and cut in very thin slices as for Julienne soup. Mix two ounces of flour in a little cold consommé, which pour into your soup with your vegetables, taking care to stir well with a spoon. Add a pinch of sugar, boil an hour, skim, and serve.

48. **Giblet Soup of Goose.** Take the giblets of a goose, which cut in small pieces. Singe and remove the skin from the feet, and cut them in small pieces, as also four ounces of larding pork. Put all together in a saucepan, with one ounce of butter, and, when beginning to color brown, add two ounces of flour, and boil for five minutes. Then add three pints of consommé (stock), two green onions, a very little thyme, a clove of garlic, two cloves, a bay-leaf, and a little mace, around which put a few branches of parsley, and tie all together. Carefully remove all grease from your soup, add a wineglass of sherry, and serve.

49. **Soup à la Bohemienne.** Cut a carrot in very small pieces, which put in a saucepan with an ounce of butter. When beginning to color lightly, add three pints of consommé (stock, Art. 1), boil for half an hour, skim, add a pint of peas, a pinch of sugar, pepper, and nutmeg. When your peas are cooked, make a paste with three ounces of flour, two yolks of eggs, one

whole egg, a glass of cream, and a little salt and nutmeg. Put through a sieve into your soup, which must be boiling on the fire, stir with a spoon, boil for ten minutes, add a tablespoonful of chopped parsley, and serve.

50. **Soup with Poached Eggs à la Styrie.** Take three pints of consommé (stock, Art. 1), which boil, and add thereto, by degrees, two ounces of semolina, stirring constantly with a spoon. Poach in boiling water with a little salt, and a tablespoonful of vinegar, six eggs, which put into cold water. Blanch a tablespoonful of chopped parsley, which add to your soup, with three quarters of a pint of green peas, and, lastly, your poached eggs, which, just before serving in your soup, place in hot water for an instant.

51. **English Hare Soup.** Cut a young hare in small pieces, which put in a saucepan with four ounces of lard, cut in small squares, two ounces of butter, and, when beginning to color brown, add one ounce of flour, half a bottle of claret, and a quart of consommé (stock, Art. 1). Season with a little thyme, a bay-leaf, two onions, a dozen mushrooms, two cloves, a little salt, pepper, mace, and a very little cayenne. Boil, and then remove your saucepan to the back of the range to simmer gently. Take off all grease most carefully, and, when your hare is thoroughly done, strain your consommé and serve with the hare.

52. **Soup of Sturgeon à la Pierre Legrand.** Take one pound of pike, one of perch, and the same of eels, which put into a saucepan, with an onion cut in slices, a carrot, a clove of garlic, a very little thyme, and a bay-leaf. Cut up your fish, add four wineglasses of sherry, boil until all moisture is absorbed, add three pints of consommé (stock, Art. 1 ), boil for one hour, and press through a sieve. Take two pounds of sturgeon, and boil gently with a carrot, an onion, a slice of ham, salt, pepper, a small garlic, a pint of consommé, and a glass of sherry. Make a farce of quenelles (see Art. 11), form in small balls, which poach in hot water. Add them to the slices of sturgeon, also the ends of a bunch of asparagus, previously boiled, and two tablespoonfuls of chervil, chopped very fine. Strain the liquid in which your sturgeon was boiled, add to the essence of fish prepared above, boil for a few moments, and serve.

53. **Clam Chowder à la Thayer.** Put half a pound of fat salt pork in a saucepan, let it fry slowly, and then remove it from the fire and put it aside

to cool. Chop up fine fifty large hard-clams, also half a can of tomatoes, a handful of celery, the same of parsley, a quart of onions, half a dozen pilot-biscuit, a little thyme, and two quarts of potatoes cut up in pieces about as large as a five-cent piece. Put the saucepan in which you have your pork again on the fire, add first the onions, and then the other ingredients, with the juice of the clams, and enough water to cover. Add black pepper, a little salt, and an eighth of a pint of Worcestershire sauce. Stir from the bottom so as to avoid burning, and simmer gently until the potatoes are thoroughly done. When the chowder begins to boil, you may add boiling water if you find it too thick. Five minutes before serving, add half a lemon sliced thin.

54. **OllaPodrida** (Spanish Soup). Put in a saucepan two pounds of beef, a pint of dwarf or chick peas, which you have previously soaked in water for six hours. Then blanch in boiling water for twenty minutes half a pound of bacon and half a pound of raw ham, which add to the other ingredients, with enough water to cover them. Skim carefully, and, after boiling gently two hours, add a fowl, a carrot, an onion, a clove of garlic, two cloves, and two bay-leaves, which inclose in some branches of parsley, tying all together. Boil again for an hour, adding two smoked sausages (choricos), which may be found at any Italian grocery, and a cabbage previously blanched. Continue boiling gently for two hours; soak a pinch of saffron in water, strain it into your soup on the fire, and boil thirty minutes longer, until the ingredients become yellow. Strain your soup, remove the meats, drain, arrange as neatly as possible on a dish, and serve with the soup.

55. **Bouillabaisse à la Marseillaise.** Put into a saucepan an onion chopped very fine, with a tablespoonful of oil. When beginning to color slightly, cut in slices half a pound of pike, the same of perch, flounder, eel, and lobster, which wash and clean well. Place them in a saucepan with parsley, two chopped cloves of garlic, some pepper and salt, a little nutmeg, and a pinch of saffron, which mix in two tablespoonfuls of water, and strain into your saucepan. Moisten with three pints of fish-broth (see [Art. 4](#)), two tablespoonfuls of oil, and a wineglass of sherry. Boil on a quick fire for twenty minutes. Take some rather thick pieces of bread, over which pour the liquid in which your fish was boiled, and serve the fish on a separate dish.

## PURÉES.

56. **Purée of Sorrel.** Proceed as for clear sorrel soup (Art. 12), except with the addition of four yolks of eggs, mixed in a little water, just before serving the soup and when it has entirely ceased boiling. Serve with it some square pieces of bread fried in butter.

57. **Cream of Sorrel.** Boil one quart of sorrel, drain it, put it in cold water, and press it through a sieve. Put it in a saucepan with not quite a quart of consommé (stock), and the same of cream; salt, pepper, and an ounce of butter. Boil for a few moments, and then remove the saucepan to the back of the range. When it has ceased boiling, take the yolks of four eggs, which mix in a little water; add to your soup, and serve.

58. **Purée of Green Peas.** Take a quart of green peas and put them in a saucepan with boiling water, adding some parsley and a little salt. Boil rapidly, until the peas are thoroughly done, then drain them and remove the parsley. Pound them, and press them through a sieve, and return them to the fire, in a saucepan, with a pint and a half of consommé and the same of cream. When boiling, add an ounce of butter, a little salt, a pinch of sugar, and serve with small squares of bread fried in butter.

59. **Purée of Peas à la Princesse.** Boil a chicken in a little more than three pints of consommé (stock, Art. 1). If an ordinary chicken, it will take forty minutes; if an old one, two hours. After it is done, let it become cold, and cut it in pieces to serve in your soup. Make the purée of peas like the preceding; add to it the consommé in which the chicken was cooked, and serve with small squares of bread fried in butter.

60. **Split-Pea Soup.** Take a pint of split peas, which, having washed well, place in a saucepan with an onion, a clove, half an ounce of ham, and two quarts of cold water. Boil until the peas are very soft, press them through a sieve, put them again on the fire, with the addition of an ounce of butter, three pints of consommé (stock, Art. 1), and serve with some small pieces of bread fried in butter.

61. **Purée of Lentils.** Take a quart of lentils, wash them well, and put them in a saucepan with a slice of lean ham, the carcass of a partridge, a carrot, an onion, a few branches of parsley, a few pieces of celery, and add three pints of consommé (stock). Boil until the lentils are thoroughly cooked, drain, remove the ham, partridge, and parsley, press through a

sieve, place on the fire again, adding one ounce of butter, boil for a moment, and serve with small squares of bread fried in butter.

62. **Purée of White Beans.** Take one pint of white beans, which wash well, and boil thoroughly in three pints of consommé (stock, Art. 1). When the beans are done, press them through a sieve, put them again on the fire, adding one ounce of butter, a pinch of sugar, boil for a moment, and serve with small squares of bread fried in butter. This soup can be varied by adding a plateful of string-beans boiled separately with a little salt and a very little soda, after which put in cold water for a moment, and then cut in diamonds. Chop a teaspoonful of parsley, and serve with the string-beans in your soup.

63. **Purée of Asparagus.** Take a bunch of asparagus, separate the heads from the stalks, wash them, and then boil them with a little salt and a very little soda, after which put them in cold water for a moment. Put into a saucepan one ounce of butter, two ounces of flour, a little salt, a pinch of sugar, and add the heads of asparagus, a pint and a half of cream, the same of consommé (stock, Art. 1). Stir all together until boiling, strain, put back on the fire for a few moments, and, adding an ounce of butter, serve.

64. **Purée of Rice.** Take half a pound of rice, which wash well in several waters, boil for a few moments, then put in cold water, drain, and place in a saucepan with one quart of consommé (stock), and boil for about an hour. Press through a sieve, and put back on the fire until it begins to boil, then add one pint of cream and an ounce of butter; serve.

65. **Rice Soup à la Crécy.** Take two very red carrots, a turnip, and an onion, which cut in slices, and a clove. Boil these in not quite a quart of consommé (stock, Art. 1) for about an hour. Press through a sieve. Then boil four ounces of rice, after which drain and put it in cold water for a moment; drain again, and boil for three quarters of an hour in nearly a quart of consommé. Add the purée of vegetables, and, when beginning to boil up again, add one ounce of butter, and serve.

66. **Purée of Barley.** Take half a pound of barley, which boil for about five minutes, then put in cold water. Drain, and add it to three pints of consommé (stock, Art. 1), boil about two hours, press through a sieve and

put back on the fire until it begins to boil, adding one ounce of butter and two tablespoonfuls of green peas, previously boiled; serve.

67. **Purée of Celery.** Take a bunch of celery, and wash it well; cut it in pieces and place it in a saucepan with water, a little salt, and boil thoroughly, drain, and put it in cold water. In another saucepan put an ounce of butter (which melt), one ounce of flour, salt, pepper, and a very little nutmeg; mix all together, adding the celery, not quite a quart of consommé (stock), and the same of cream. Put it on the fire, taking care to stir until it boils, press through a sieve and again put it on the fire for a moment; serve.

68. **Purée Soubise à la Princesse.** Blanch six onions in boiling water, with a little salt, until they become soft. Drain and dry them in a napkin. Then put them in a saucepan with an ounce of butter, on a very gentle fire, so that they may only color slightly; add two ounces of flour, a little salt, pepper, and a very little nutmeg; moisten with a pint and a half of consommé (stock, [Art. 1](#)), and the same of cream. When beginning to boil, press through a sieve, heat again on the fire, adding half an ounce of butter, and serve.

69. **Purée of Potatoes à la Jackson.** Bake in the oven half a dozen potatoes. Take out the inside, which put in a saucepan with an ounce of butter. Mix thoroughly together with a spoon, and season with a little salt, pepper, a pinch of sugar, and a very little nutmeg. Moisten with a pint and a half of consommé (stock), press through a sieve, put back on the fire, and as soon as beginning to boil add a pint and a half of cream; heat without boiling, then add four yolks of eggs well mixed in a little water, and serve.

70. **Purée of Jerusalem Artichokes.** Clean a dozen Jerusalem artichokes, cut them in pieces, and put them in a saucepan with a little butter, salt, and a pinch of sugar. As soon as they begin to color slightly, add a pint and a half of consommé (stock, [Art. 1](#)), boil a little longer, and press through a sieve. Put back on the fire until beginning to boil, add an ounce of butter, a pint and a half of cream, and when very hot, without boiling, add the yolks of four eggs, which you have previously mixed well in a little water. You may serve with small squares of bread fried in butter if desired.

71. **Purée of Fowl à la Reine.** Clean a chicken, and put it in a saucepan with a quart of consommé (stock, [Art. 1](#)), a carrot, an onion, and a clove.

Simmer very gently for three hours; take out the fowl, cut off the white meat, and pound very fine. Remove the grease carefully from your soup in which the fowl has been cooked, then add the pounded chicken, and put through a sieve. Heat it up again on the fire, add a pint and a half of cream, taking care that it does not boil, add very little nutmeg, pepper, salt, a very little sugar, an ounce of butter, and the yolks of four eggs, well mixed in a little water. Serve.

72. **Purée of Partridge.** Remove the shells of two dozen French chestnuts, which boil five minutes, remove the skins, and put the chestnuts in a saucepan with a little salt and water, and boil for about five minutes. Cut off all the meat from a cold partridge, which pound in a mortar, together with the chestnuts, and then press through a sieve. Boil the bones of your partridge for about half an hour in three pints of consommé (stock, Art. 1), adding a wineglass of sherry, strain, and add it to your chestnuts and partridge. Put in a saucepan two tablespoonfuls of flour, with an ounce of butter, a little pepper, and salt. Mix all well together, and add them to your purée, which should be very hot. When economy is no object, you may add two partridges instead of one, which will give a better flavor to your purée, to which, if you find too thick, you may add a little more consommé.

73. **Purée of Rabbit.** Remove the fillets from an uncooked rabbit, and place them in a saucepan on a moderate fire, with half an ounce of butter, and simmer very gently. In another saucepan put the remainder of the rabbit with an onion, a clove, and a little nutmeg, and three pints of consommé (stock, Art. 1). Simmer gently three quarters of an hour, remove the meat from the thighs and shoulders, pound it together with two ounces of rice well boiled, moisten with the consommé in which your rabbit was cooked, and put through a sieve. Cut your fillets of rabbit, which you cooked in butter, into small pieces, and serve in your soup.

74. **TomatoSoup.** Cut a carrot and an onion in slices, add a slice of raw ham and a clove, and put into a saucepan with half an ounce of butter. As soon as your vegetables begin to color slightly, mix well with them an ounce of flour, add a quart of tomatoes, and boil for thirty minutes. Strain, then season with salt and pepper, put again on the fire, add a pint of consommé (stock), and boil for five minutes, and add an ounce of butter.

Remove the grease from your soup, and serve with small squares of bread fried in butter.

75. **Purée of Vegetables aux Croûtons.** Clean and cut in slices a medium-sized carrot, a turnip, an onion, a leek, some pieces of celery, and add two cloves. Boil them for a few moments, and afterward put them into cold water for a moment. Then place your vegetables in a saucepan, with four ounces of dried peas, moisten with three pints consommé (or stock, Art. 1), boil for two hours, season with a little pepper, salt, and a pinch of sugar. Press through a sieve, put again on the fire with an ounce of butter, and serve in your soup, with small squares of bread fried in butter.

76. **Rice Soup au Lait d'Amandes.** Wash in cold water four ounces of rice, which boil for ten minutes, afterward put it in cold water, drain, then place it in a saucepan with three pints of milk, and boil very gently for forty-five minutes. Take four ounces of bitter-almonds with one of sweet, blanch them and pound them well, adding by degrees, as you pound, a glass of cold milk. Put through a sieve, add a pinch of salt and about a coffee-spoonful of sugar, and then with the rice and milk boil for a moment, and serve.

77. **Bisque of Crawfish.** Wash four dozen crawfish and put them in sufficient water to cover them, cut a carrot, an onion, and three cloves of garlic in slices, add two cloves, a few branches of parsley, a little salt, and a tablespoonful of vinegar, and boil for fifteen minutes. Drain them, and then pound them to a paste. Melt one ounce of butter in a saucepan, add two ounces of flour, which mix well with the butter. Then add the paste of crawfish, not quite a quart of cream, the same of consommé (stock), three quarters of a cupful of tomatoes, salt and pepper, and a little cayenne. Boil, and stir with a spoon, press through a sieve, and put back on the fire, with one ounce of butter; as soon as it boils up again, serve.

78. **Bisque of Lobster.** Take half a pound of boiled lobster from which you have removed the shell, and proceed as for the foregoing, adding half instead of three quarters of a cupful of tomatoes.

79. **Bisque of Clams.** Boil fifty clams in their juice for about five minutes, drain them, chop them fine, then pound them. Put in a saucepan on the fire four ounces of butter, with two ounces of flour, add your clams with

their juice, two pinches of salt, one of pepper, one of cayenne, and two and a half pints of milk, stir constantly, and, just before beginning to boil, remove from the fire, strain, heat again over the fire, and serve.

Bisque of oysters is prepared in the same manner.

# CHAPTER II.
## *SAUCES.*

80. **Spanish Sauce.** Melt two ounces of butter in a saucepan, to which add two ounces of flour, and put on a gentle fire, stirring until colored a nice brown; then mix with the flour and butter a pint of consommé (stock, Art. 1), an ounce and a half of lean raw ham, a carrot, an onion, a piece of celery, two cloves, a pinch of salt and pepper, and stir until beginning to boil. Remove the saucepan to the back of the range, so as to simmer gently for an hour; skim off the grease carefully and strain.

81. **Sauce Allemande.** Melt two ounces of butter and mix thoroughly with it two ounces of flour on a gentle fire. Add immediately a pint of consommé (stock, Art. 1), a little salt and pepper, and stir until boiling. After boiling fifteen minutes, remove from the fire and skim the grease off carefully. When your sauce has ceased boiling, add the yolks of three eggs, well mixed in a little water, and stirred in quickly with an egg-beater, so as to make your sauce light.

82. **Sauce Veloutée.** Put in a saucepan two pounds of veal, the thighs of a chicken, two carrots, two onions, a few branches of parsley, inclosing two cloves, two bay-leaves, a clove of garlic; tie all together, adding a little salt and pepper, and one quart of consommé (stock, Art. 1). When beginning to boil, skim constantly, so as to clear the sauce well. Remove the saucepan to the back of the range and simmer gently two hours. Melt two ounces of butter in a saucepan on the fire, with which mix thoroughly an ounce of flour. When beginning to color slightly, add a pint of the liquid in which your meats were boiled, strain half a wineglass of the juice of canned mushrooms, add it to your sauce, which boil forty-five minutes; strain, and serve.

83. **Béchamel Sauce.** Melt an ounce of butter in a saucepan, add an ounce of flour, and mix well together. Then add an onion cut in slices, half an ounce of lean raw ham, and a little salt and pepper. When beginning to

color slightly, moisten with a pint of milk, stir well until boiling, after which boil ten minutes longer; strain, and serve.

84. **White Sauce, or Butter-Sauce.** Put in a saucepan on the fire an ounce of butter, which melt, and add to it one tablespoonful of flour, a little salt, white pepper, a little nutmeg, and mix all well together, adding a glass of water; stir until boiling, add an ounce of butter and the juice of a lemon; strain, and serve.

85. **Sauce Hollandaise.** Put two ounces of butter in a saucepan, with a little salt, nutmeg, a glass and a quarter of water, and mix all together on the fire. Put into another saucepan two tablespoonfuls of vinegar, which reduce one half; add it to your other ingredients, with a tablespoonful of Béchamel sauce (Art. 83), and an ounce of butter, mixing all well together. Take the yolks of four eggs, which mix in a little water, and, removing your sauce from the fire, when it has ceased boiling, add the eggs, the juice of a lemon, strain, and serve.

86. **Sauce Piquante.** Chop four shallots very fine, put them in a saucepan with four tablespoonfuls of sweet-oil. When beginning to color slightly, add half a pint of Spanish sauce (Art. 80), boil slowly for a few minutes, then add two ounces of pickles, and serve.

87. **Bread-Sauce.** Chop an onion very fine, put it in a saucepan, with four ounces of bread-crumbs, which you have put through a sieve, add a little salt, pepper, and a glass of milk. Boil ten minutes, add a glass of cream, and serve.

88. **SauceBéarnaise.** Chop up three shallots and put them in a saucepan with a pinch of chervil, a branch of tarragon, a green onion, and two tablespoonfuls of vinegar. Reduce one half, and let cool; then add four ounces of butter, eight yolks of eggs, a sherry-glass of water, salt, pepper, and a very little nutmeg. Put your saucepan again on a gentle fire, stir well until the sauce thickens; strain, and serve.

89. **Parisian Sauce.** Put into a saucepan half an ounce of chopped truffles, a wineglass of sherry, some branches of parsley, inclosing a clove, a little thyme, a bay-leaf, and tie all together. Reduce one half on the fire,

put through a sieve, add half a pint of Allemande sauce (Art. 81); heat again on the fire, and serve.

90. **Tomato Sauce.** Put in a saucepan an ounce of raw ham, a carrot, an onion, very little thyme, a bay-leaf, two cloves, a clove of garlic, and half an ounce of butter. Simmer for ten minutes, add an ounce of flour well mixed in half a pint of tomatoes and a glass of consommé (stock, Art. 1). Boil for half an hour, season with a little salt, pepper, a very little nutmeg, strain, and serve.

91. **SaucePérigueux.** Chop an ounce of truffles, put them in a saucepan on the fire, with a glass of sherry and a glass of white wine. Reduce one half, then add half a pint of Spanish sauce (Art. 80 ), boil five minutes, and serve.

92. **SauceRobert.** Cut an onion in small pieces, and put it in a saucepan with half an ounce of butter. When it begins to color, drain off the butter, and moisten with half a glass of consommé (stock, Art. 1). Boil gently for thirty minutes, add half a pint of Spanish sauce (Art. 80), a wineglass of sherry, and a tablespoonful of English mustard mixed in a little water.

93. **ItalianSauce.** Peel and chop two shallots, which, with a little butter, put in a saucepan on the fire. When beginning to color slightly, moisten with half a pint of Spanish sauce (Art. 80) and a wineglass of sherry. Boil for twenty minutes. Chop half an ounce of lean, cooked ham, half a dozen mushrooms chopped fine, and a little chopped parsley. After skimming the grease from your sauce, add these ingredients, boil five minutes, and serve.

94. **SauceSoubise.** Peel and chop three onions, which put in a saucepan on the fire with an ounce of butter. Simmer very gently, so as not to color too much, and, after three quarters of an hour, add a tablespoonful of flour, salt, pepper, a little nutmeg, and mix all together. Moisten with a gill of consommé (stock, Art. 1), the same of cream, boil for five minutes, strain, heat again on the fire, and serve.

95. **Sauce Poivrade.** Put into a saucepan a chopped onion, three branches of thyme, three bay-leaves, a clove of garlic, three cloves, six pepper-corns, half an ounce of raw ham cut in small pieces, four tablespoonfuls of vinegar, a little pepper, a very little cayenne; reduce until

almost dry, moisten with a claret-glass of red wine and half a pint of Spanish sauce (Art. 80), boil fifteen minutes, strain, and serve.

96. **Sauce Hachée.** Peel and chop an onion, a pickle, a shallot, a tablespoonful of capers, and moisten with two tablespoonfuls of vinegar. Put them in a saucepan on the fire, reduce one half, add half a pint of Spanish sauce (Art. 80), a little cayenne pepper, a pinch of parsley chopped fine, half an ounce of capers, and two tablespoonfuls of wine-vinegar, boil five minutes, and serve.

97. **Hunter Sauce.** Put the remains of a roast partridge in a saucepan with half an ounce of raw ham, a carrot, an onion, a clove of garlic, a little thyme, three bay-leaves, and three cloves. Moisten with a glass of white wine, reduce one half, add half a pint of Spanish sauce (Art. 80), boil half an hour, strain, and serve.

98. **SauceColbert.** Put an ounce of glaze (Art. 179) in a saucepan on the fire with a tablespoonful of consommé (stock, Art. 1). Mix well together, and add half a pint of consommé (stock, Art. 1 ), half an ounce of butter in small pieces, and by degrees, stirring all the time. When all well mixed together, strain, add the juice of a lemon, a tablespoonful of chopped parsley, and serve.

99. **Sauce Suprême.** Cut up the remains of two roast chickens, which put into a saucepan with a pint of consommé (stock, Art. 1), some branches of parsley, inclosing a clove, a clove of garlic, two bay-leaves, salt, and white pepper, a very little thyme, and tie all together. Boil one hour, and strain. Put two ounces of butter in another saucepan, a tablespoonful of flour, a teaspoonful of corn-starch, mix thoroughly together, and add the liquid in which the remains of the chicken were broiled. Stir with a spoon until boiling, reduce one quarter, pour in two wineglasses of cream and one wineglass of sherry. Boil fifteen minutes longer, add the juice of a lemon, strain, and serve.

100. **SauceVenétienne.** Put two tablespoonfuls of vinegar in a saucepan on the fire, with some parsley, a little tarragon, two cloves, a very little thyme, half an ounce of raw ham chopped up. Reduce one half, and add half a pint sauce veloutée (Art. 82). Boil five minutes and strain. Chop fine a

tablespoonful of chervil, the same of tarragon, boil them in hot water five minutes, dry with a napkin, and add to your sauce just before serving.

101. **Sauce Bordelaise.** Peel two cloves of garlic, and put them in a saucepan, with a pinch of chervil, a few tarragon-leaves, two bay-leaves, a lemon, from which you have removed the peel and the seeds, two cloves, two tablespoonfuls of oil, and two claret-glasses of white wine. Reduce one half on a very gentle fire, add half a pint of Spanish sauce ([Art. 80](Art. 80)), boil half an hour, carefully remove all grease, and pour in another glass of white wine. Boil ten minutes, add the juice of a lemon, strain, put back your sauce on the fire, cut a dozen mushrooms in very small pieces, add them to your sauce, and serve.

102. **Another way of making Sauce Bordelaise.** Peel and chop very fine four cloves of garlic, which put into a saucepan with three tablespoonfuls of oil. When beginning to color lightly, add a tablespoonful of chopped parsley. This sauce should never be made until ready to serve on the instant.

103. **Sauce à la Poulette.** Put in a saucepan three sherry-glasses of water, three ounces of butter, the juice of half a lemon, and a pinch of salt and white pepper. As soon as beginning to boil, take off the fire, and, when boiling ceases, add the yolks of four eggs which you have previously mixed well, in about a sherry-glass of water. Stir constantly so that the sauce does not break, strain it, and add to it a little parsley chopped fine.

104. **Sauce Fleurette.** Proceed as for the foregoing, except, instead of the parsley, add only the ends of some chervil-leaves, not chopped.

105. **Sauce à la Marinière.** Cut a small eel and a pike in small pieces, put them in a saucepan, with an onion, a carrot, three branches of parsley, half a dozen mushrooms, a little thyme, two bay-leaves, and a pinch of allspice; moisten with half a bottle of red wine, and boil forty minutes. Add half a pint of Spanish sauce ([Art. 80](Art. 80)), and simmer at the back of the range for half an hour. Take out your pieces of fish and strain the liquid in which they were boiled. Peel twenty small white onions, which put in a saucepan with half an ounce of butter. When they begin to color slightly, add to them a very little of the sauce until they are cooked, then add to them the whole of the sauce, and serve.

106. **LobsterSauce.** Take a boiled lobster, separate it in two, remove the coral, which wash well in cold water; lay it on a table, with half an ounce of butter, mix well together with the blade of a knife, and press through a sieve. Pound to a paste quarter of a pound of the meat of the lobster. Put half a pint of white sauce (Art. 84) in a saucepan, and, when boiling, add the above ingredients, which stir well, so as to mix thoroughly; strain, and serve. As there is not always coral in every lobster, it is well to preserve it in a little vinegar, and put it by until needed.

107. **Shrimp Sauce.** Take half a pint of white sauce (Art. 84), which should be boiling; add a little lobster-coral and butter, as described in lobster sauce (Art. 106), or half a tablespoonful of anchovy sauce. Remove the shells from four dozen shrimps, and serve in your sauce.

108. **SauceGénevoise.** Cut a medium-sized pike in pieces, which put in a saucepan with half an ounce of raw ham cut in small pieces, two cloves, two bay-leaves, a clove of garlic, a little thyme, a pinch of salt and pepper, a few mushrooms chopped up, and two claret-glasses of red wine. Reduce one half, add half a pint of Spanish sauce (Art. 80), boil thirty minutes; then add a wineglass of madeira (or sherry); strain, and stir thoroughly into your sauce a teaspoonful of anchovy sauce.

109. **Sauce Remoulade (cold).** Put in a bowl two yolks of eggs, a tablespoonful of mustard, salt, and pepper. Mix well with the foregoing two tablespoonfuls of vinegar, and then, stirring constantly, eight tablespoonfuls of oil; and, lastly, another tablespoonful of vinegar; then chop a shallot, some chervil, some tarragon-leaves, and mix them with your sauce.

110. **Sauce Remoulade (hot).** Peel and chop very fine six shallots and a clove of garlic; put them into a saucepan with five tablespoonfuls of vinegar, and reduce on the fire one half. Pound the yolks of four hard-boiled eggs, which mix well with a teaspoonful of anchovy sauce; add to them half a pint of sauce Allemande (Art. 81) and a quarter of a tablespoonful of sweet-oil, and then the shallots, garlic, and vinegar; heat without boiling, and add a pinch of tarragon, the same of chervil and of parsley all chopped fine, a little salt and pepper, and, just before serving, two tablespoonfuls of vinegar.

111. **Sauce Ravigote (hot).** Put into a saucepan half a pint of consommé (stock, Art. 1), half a teaspoonful of vinegar, a *very little* green garlic, and the same of tarragon-leaves and chervil. Boil ten minutes, drain your herbs, press all moisture from them with a cloth, and then chop them very fine. Put on a table half an ounce of flour, and the same of butter, which mix well together and add them to your consommé and vinegar, which you have put back on the fire; stir well with a spoon until boiling, then skim the sauce, add your chopped herbs, and serve.

112. **Sauce Ravigote (cold).** Take half a pint of sauce Mayonnaise (Art. 113), to which add a little chervil, parsley, tarragon, all mashed and chopped fine, and mix well with your Mayonnaise; also a tablespoonful of mustard, and a tablespoonful of capers.

113. **Sauce Mayonnaise.** Put the yolks of two eggs in a bowl with salt, pepper, the juice of a lemon, and half a teaspoonful of dry mustard. Stir with a wooden spoon, and add by degrees, in *very* small quantities, and stirring continuously, a tablespoonful of vinegar; then, a few drops at a time, some good oil, stirring rapidly all the time, until your sauce thickens, and half a pint of oil has been absorbed.

114. **Sauce Tartare.** Proceed as for the foregoing, except that, instead of half a teaspoonful of mustard, add three. Chop a pickle and a tablespoonful of capers, which dry in a napkin. Also chop a green onion, some chervil, a few tarragon-leaves, and mix with your sauce.

# CHAPTER III.
## *FISH.*

115. **Boiled Striped Bass à la Venétienne.** Clean a striped bass of about four pounds. Cut off the fins with a scissors. Then wash your fish well, put it in a fish-kettle with four ounces of salt, and enough water to cover the fish. Simmer gently, and when beginning to boil remove it to the back of the range, to simmer for half an hour. Then serve with a sauce Venétienne (Art. 100).

116. **Boiled Red Snapper with Butter Sauce.** Proceed as for the foregoing, and serve with a white sauce (Art. 84).

117. **Boiled Salmon, Madeira Sauce.** Boil four pounds of salmon as in Art. 115, adding half a bottle of white wine, then serve with Spanish sauce (Art. 80), adding a glass of madeira or sherry. Salmon may also be served with the following sauces: Italian sauce (Art. 93), sauce Hollandaise (Art. 85), sauce Génevoise (Art. 108), or cold with sauce Tartare (Art. 114), sauce ravigote (Art. 112), or sauce remoulade (Art. 109).

118. **Halibut, Lobster Sauce.** Boil four pounds of halibut, and serve with a lobster sauce (Art. 106).

119. **Boiled Codfish, Oyster Sauce.** Boil a codfish. Stew two dozen oysters, which drain, and add to a white sauce (Art. 84). Boiled codfish may also be served with caper sauce, sauce Hollandaise (Art. 85), and other white sauces.

120. **Sheep's Head, Shrimp Sauce.** Boil a sheep's head, and serve with a shrimp sauce (Art. 107 ).

121. **Salmon-Trout, Sauce Hollandaise.** Boil a salmon-trout, and serve with sauce Hollandaise (Art. 85).

122. **Pickerel, Anchovy Sauce.** Clean a pickerel of four pounds and put it in a fish-kettle with enough water to cover it; add four ounces of salt, a

carrot cut in slices, an onion, six branches of thyme, six cloves, six peppercorns, some parsley-roots, and a tablespoonful of vinegar. When beginning to boil remove the fish-kettle to the back of the range for about half an hour. Take half a pint of Spanish sauce (Art. 80), into which mix two teaspoonfuls of anchovy sauce, and, when boiling, serve with your fish.

123. **Black Bass, Burgundy Sauce.** Clean a black bass of four pounds, put it in the fish-kettle to boil, adding half a bottle of claret. Then let it simmer for half an hour at the back of the range. Take half a pint of Spanish sauce (Art. 80), put it in a saucepan with two wineglasses of red wine, reduce one quarter, and serve with your fish.

124. **Baked Blue-Fish, Tomato Sauce.** Clean a blue-fish of four pounds and place it in a buttered pan. Cover the fish with tomato sauce (Art. 90), on top of which put some bread-crumbs and a few little pieces of butter. Place in the oven for about forty minutes, or until you see that the flesh is detached from the backbone, and serve with tomato sauce around it.

125. **Baked Fillet of Sole (or Flounder).** Cut a flounder of four pounds into fillets, that is, in pieces of about five inches long and four in width, tapering to a point at each end. Each piece should be not quite an inch thick. Put them in a buttered pan, cover with sauce Allemande (Art. 81), on top of which sprinkle some bread-crumbs and a few small pieces of butter. Put into the oven until well browned. Place half a pint of sauce Allemande in a saucepan, with the addition of a wineglass of sherry, boil ten minutes, pour it around your fish, and serve.

126. **Weak-Fish, Italian Sauce.** Cut a weak-fish of four pounds in fillets, as described in the foregoing, and place them in a saucepan with a little melted butter, salt, pepper, a little nutmeg, and two tablespoonfuls of madeira (or sherry). Simmer gently for twenty minutes, arrange your fish neatly on a dish, one piece overlapping the other, and serve with an Italian sauce (Art. 93).

127. **Chicken Halibut aux Fines Herbes.** Chop a little parsley, six mushrooms, and a shallot; add to them a little salt, pepper, and nutmeg, and place all together in a saucepan on the fire for five minutes, with half a pint of white wine. Then put these ingredients on a dish, and place on top of them four pounds of chicken halibut. Send to a moderate oven for about

thirty minutes, taking care from time to time to pour with a spoon some of the liquid in the dish over your fish. Put half a pint of Spanish sauce (Art. 80) in another saucepan on the fire, reduce your sauce for about seven or eight minutes, adding the juice of a lemon, and serve it around your fish.

128. **Eels à la Tartare.** Broil your eels on a gridiron. When the skin detaches itself on one side, turn them on the other. When done, with a napkin take off all the skin, cut the eels in pieces three inches long, remove the insides, and put the eels in a saucepan with a little salt, pepper, six cloves, six pepper-corns, two parsley-roots, a little thyme, four bay-leaves, and two tablespoonfuls of vinegar. Add enough water to cover your eels, and, after boiling fifteen minutes, take them off the fire, let them cool in the liquid in which they were cooked, and then wipe them dry with a cloth. Break in a bowl two eggs, which mix thoroughly with half an ounce of melted butter; pour this over your fish, and sprinkle lightly with bread-crumbs. Broil them on a very gentle fire. When they are a nice brown, serve them with a sauce Tartare (Art. 114).

129. **King-Fish, Sherry Sauce.** Clean four medium-sized king-fish, split them in two, and broil them on a gentle fire. Put half a pint of Spanish sauce (Art. 80) in a saucepan, add a wineglass of sherry, boil fifteen minutes, pour it around your fish, and serve.

130. **Fillet of Shad, with Purée of Sorrel.** After cleaning your shad, cut it in equal pieces, leaving the skin underneath. Put them on a plate, and sprinkle a little salt on them, add the juice of a lemon, and a few branches of parsley. A few moments before they are required to be served put them in a saucepan on a gentle fire for fifteen minutes, with a glass of white wine and an ounce of butter. Pick and clean a quart of sorrel, which blanch in boiling water, drain, and press it through a sieve. Put an ounce of butter in a saucepan with half an ounce of flour, a little salt, pepper, and nutmeg, and, when beginning to color slightly, add your purée of sorrel and half a glass of cream. Simmer gently ten minutes, when add the yolks of two eggs which you have mixed in a little milk. Boil five minutes longer, pour over your fish, and serve.

131. **Broiled Shad à la Maître d'Hôtel.** Clean a shad, without removing the skin, split it in two, and put the roes on a buttered pan, which send to the

oven until brown. Then broil the shad, and when done put it on a dish together with the roes. Melt an ounce of butter, in which put a little salt and pepper, a little chopped parsley, and the juice of a lemon. Mix well together, pour over your shad, and serve. Porgies, mackerel, and other broiling fish, may be served in the same manner.

132. **Long Island Brook-Trout.** Clean and wash a trout of about four pounds, and put it in a fish-kettle with four ounces of salt. When beginning to boil remove your fish-kettle to the back of the range for twenty-five minutes. Blanch four roes of shad in a little boiling water and a little salt, drain, and cut them in small pieces, as also a dozen mushrooms. Add these, with the juice of a lemon, to a pint of sauce Allemande (Art. 81), and boil ten minutes. Serve the fish garnished with sprigs of parsley, and the sauce in a separate dish.

133. **Trout à la Génevoise.** Clean four little trout, cut off the gills, and put your fish in an earthen pot for four hours, with a little thyme, four bay-leaves, two shallots cut in pieces, five branches of parsley, a little pepper and salt, and the juice of two lemons, after which drain, and place them in a saucepan on the fire, with a chopped onion, a clove of garlic, and a little nutmeg. Add enough red wine to cover your fish, and boil gently for twenty minutes. Take half a pint of Spanish sauce (Art. 80), boil for about an hour with one half of the liquid in which the foregoing ingredients were boiled. Chop four mushrooms and truffles, a little parsley, and add to your sauce. Put your fish on a dish, garnish with parsley, and serve with your sauce on a separate dish.

134. **Scallops of Trout.** Prepare as the foregoing a medium-sized trout, which cut in round pieces, or in the shape of an egg, and about three inches in length, and put into a saucepan in which you have previously melted two ounces of butter; add a little salt, white pepper, the juice of a lemon; and when they are done on one side, turn them on the other; mash some potatoes, and with them form a border on a plate, which may go to the oven. Moisten your potatoes lightly with some melted butter, and send them to the oven to brown. When done, arrange your scallops of fish in the middle of the potatoes, and pour over all a sauce béchamel (Art. 83).

135. **Halibut, Sauce Suprême.** Take four pounds of halibut, which cut in square pieces; soak them for an hour in four wineglasses of madeira (or sherry); turn them over from time to time, first on one side and then on the other. Just before serving, put them into a saucepan, in which you have melted two ounces of butter; add a little salt and pepper, put them on the fire for a few moments, and then send to the oven for twenty minutes. Arrange your fish on a dish, and pour over them a sauce suprême ([Art. 99](Art. 99)).

136. **Scallops of White-Fish à la Provençale.** Cut a white-fish of four pounds into round pieces, or in the shape of an egg, and about three inches in length; put them in a dish with a clove of garlic, a little thyme, three bay-leaves, two roots of parsley, an onion cut in thin slices, salt and pepper, and moisten them with a sherry-glass of oil: then peel three white onions, which cut in slices, blanch them in boiling water, with a little salt; drain them and put them in a frying-pan on the fire, with a wineglass of oil, which heat thoroughly, and, when beginning to color slightly, drain off the oil, and moisten with half a bottle of white wine. Then drain your fish, which put in the saucepan with your onions. Simmer gently for thirty minutes, drain, and in the liquor in which your fish was cooked put a tablespoonful of tomato sauce, reduce gently about one third, pour over your fish, and serve.

137. **Eels en Matelote.** Clean an eel, a pike, and a perch; cut them in slices; place them in a saucepan with a clove of garlic, two bay-leaves, two branches of thyme, three cloves, a little basil, and a few branches of parsley; add enough red wine to cover your fish. Put them on a very gentle fire, and, when beginning to boil, add a wineglass of brandy. Shake gently, so as not to break your fish, and, after boiling fifteen minutes, drain off your fish, and keep them hot. Put on a table half an ounce of flour and an ounce of butter; mix well together with the blade of a knife, and add to the liquid in which your fish was boiled. Peel and press through a sieve twenty small white onions, which put in a frying-pan, with a little butter, on a very gentle fire; add them, with a dozen mushrooms, to your fish, which heat up again. Take the ingredients in which your fish was first cooked, and place them in a dish, your fish on top. Garnish with some boiled crawfish, and some pieces of bread cut in triangles, and fried in butter.

138. **Red Snapper à la Chambord.** Take a red snapper, about four pounds in weight. Remove the scales, and on one side of the fish cut a

square in the skin, which take out, and in the flesh insert two dozen pieces of truffles, cut in squares, and pointed at one end. Over this tie a thin piece of larding pork. Put your fish in a fish-kettle, surround it with a sliced carrot and onion, three cloves of garlic, six bay-leaves, six cloves, six branches of thyme, four parsley-roots, and cover the fish with half a bottle of white wine and a quart of consommé (stock, Art. 1); put it on the fire until boiling, and then send it to a gentle oven to cook slowly for an hour, basting it often with its own liquor, on the side studded with truffles. Take half a pint of Spanish sauce (Art. 80), to which add two wineglasses of the liquid in which your fish was cooked, put your sauce on the fire to boil, skim off the grease, and strain; then put it back again on the fire for a few moments, adding a dozen mushrooms, a dozen quenelles (Art. 11), as many truffles cut in quarters, a dozen crawfish, and the same of chicken's kidneys which you have previously blanched in hot water, with a little salt, for ten minutes. Lay your fish on a dish, pour your sauce around it, and serve.

139. **Ray, with Caper Sauce.** Cook your fish as the foregoing, with the exception of the truffles, and serve with it a white sauce (Art. 84), to which add some capers.

140. **Ray, au Beurre Noir.** Cut in moderate-sized pieces four pounds of ray-fish, which put in a saucepan with an onion cut in slices, three parsley-roots, four cloves, six pepper-corns, half an ounce of salt, and four tablespoonfuls of vinegar. When beginning to boil, put your saucepan at the back of the range for thirty minutes, so as not to boil. Then take off the skin from both sides of your fish, which put in the saucepan with your other ingredients to keep hot. Put in a frying-pan four ounces of butter, and, when colored black, fry a dozen sprigs of parsley for a moment, remove them, and add to your butter two tablespoonfuls of vinegar. Strain your fish, which arrange on a dish, garnish with the fried parsley, pour the black butter over the fish, and serve.

141. **Fried Smelts.** Clean about two dozen smelts, cut off the gills, wash them well in cold water, and dry them thoroughly. Put a pinch of salt and pepper in a little milk, into which dip your smelts, and then roll them in flour. Put in a frying-pan about a pound and a half of lard, in which, when very hot, fry your smelts a light brown. Also fry some parsley, which place around your fish, and serve with a sauce Tartare (Art. 112).

142. **Farcied Smelts.** Prepare your smelts as the foregoing. Split them in two, taking care to make the opening in the under part of the fish, and, beginning at the tail, make the incision the length of the fish, without disturbing the head. Then take some chicken farce ([Art. 11](#)), and add to it half a dozen very finely chopped mushrooms, and a very little chopped parsley. Lay this on one side of your smelts, and cover with the other half. Place them in a buttered pan, cover each one with a very little melted butter, sprinkle some bread-crumbs lightly over them, and send them to the oven for about fifteen minutes. Take half a pint of Spanish sauce ([Art. 80](#)), add a sherry-glass of white wine, boil for fifteen minutes, add a little chopped parsley to your sauce, which pour over your fish, and serve.

143. **Oysters à la Poulette.** Take fifty oysters, which blanch in boiling water, then drain them, preserving part of the liquid in which they were boiled. Take half a pint of béchamel sauce ([Art. 83](#) ), add a little of the liquid in which your oysters were boiled, a little salt and pepper, a little chopped parsley, and, when your sauce has ceased boiling, the yolks of three eggs well mixed in a little water. Serve your oysters hot in the sauce.

144. **Farcied Oysters à l'Africaine.** Take twenty very large oysters, which blanch and then drain. Also take some chicken farce ([Art. 11](#)), chopping three truffles very fine, and mix with your farce, with which cover your oysters on both sides, and dip in bread-crumbs. Then beat up four eggs, the yolks and whites together, with a little salt, pepper, and very little nutmeg added, and spread over your oysters, which dip again into bread-crumbs. Put the oysters in a buttered pan, and send to the oven for about fifteen minutes, a very little melted butter on each oyster. Take half a pint of Spanish sauce ([Art. 80](#)), add to it a glass of sherry, and, after boiling twenty minutes, chop up two truffles, put them in your sauce, and serve with your oysters.

145. **Fried Oysters.** Take fifty large oysters, dip them in beaten eggs, in which you have put a little salt and pepper; then roll them in bread-crumbs, and, if your oysters should not be very large, dip them again in beaten eggs, and again roll them in bread-crumbs. Fry them in very hot lard, drain off the grease, and serve very hot. Garnish with slices of lemon.

146. **Broiled Oysters.** Take fifty large oysters, which drain and dip in four beaten eggs, to which you have added a little salt and pepper. Roll them in bread-crumbs, dip them again in eggs, and again roll them in bread-crumbs. Put a few drops of melted butter on each, broil them on a gridiron a light brown, and serve very hot.

147. **Cromesqui of Oysters.** Boil fifty oysters for about five minutes, drain them, and chop them fine. Put in a saucepan on the fire an ounce of butter, the same of flour, a pinch of salt, the same of pepper and nutmeg, and mix all well together. Add the juice of your oysters, and half a glass of milk, and stir with a wooden spoon until just before beginning to boil, then remove it from the fire; add two yolks of eggs mixed in about a tablespoonful of water, and then your oysters. Put this mixture on ice until cold, form it into balls about the size of a small egg, and wrap up each one in a very thin piece of pork. Break three eggs in a bowl, add six ounces of flour, and a little water, so as to make a smooth and very soft paste, but sufficiently solid to adhere to your cromesqui. Then mix a teaspoonful of soda with your paste, with which cover each one, and fry in very hot lard. When a bright yellow, drain, and serve hot.

148. **Oysters on Toast.** Put fifty oysters in a frying-pan with their liquor, toss them on the fire for about ten minutes, and sprinkle with chopped parsley. Put the oysters on eight pieces of toast, the juice poured over them. Serve very hot.

149. **Oysters a la Mosely.** Take fifty oysters, the third of which put in a deep dish with a little pepper, salt, a little melted butter, and cover with bread-crumbs. Then put half of the remaining oysters on top. Proceed as above, add a third layer, pour in enough sherry to reach the top of your oysters, cover with bread-crumbs, and a little melted butter, and send to a moderate oven until colored a light brown. Serve very hot.

150. **Oysters au Gratin.** Take three dozen rather small oysters, blanch them, and drain them. Make a rather thick béchamel sauce ([Art. 83](#)), to which add two yolks of eggs well mixed in a little water. When beginning to boil, add your oysters, a little salt, pepper, and a little nutmeg. Mix all well together, and then put them, with your sauce, in the shells. Cover them

lightly with bread-crumbs, and a few drops of melted butter on top. Send them to the oven, and serve when nicely browned.

151. **Lobster au Naturel.** Put in a saucepan two sliced onions, a few green onions, some parsley, four cloves, four branches of thyme, one of sage, a pinch of mace, a little piece of green pepper, two ounces of salt, and enough water to cover them. Boil them for twenty minutes, and then allow them to cool, after which add four medium-sized lobsters, boil for half an hour; take them off the fire, and let them become cold in their liquor. Then drain them, split them in two, break their claws, and serve them garnished with parsley.

152. **Lobster à la Havraise.** Take three small live lobsters, cut off the claws, break them, and separate your lobsters in two, cutting each lobster in eight pieces. Put into a frying-pan three very finely chopped shallots, with a tablespoonful of oil. When beginning to color lightly, add your pieces of lobster, and, after cooking fifteen minutes, add half a pint of Spanish sauce (Art. 80), a glass of sherry, about ten mushrooms, a little chopped parsley, a little salt, pepper, and a very little nutmeg. Mix well together, boil five minutes longer, and serve.

153. **Croquettes of Lobster.** Chop fine the meat of two boiled lobsters and add half a pint of béchamel sauce (Art. 83), to which you have added the yolks of two eggs well mixed in a little water. Then add two tablespoonfuls of tomato sauce, a little pepper, salt, and a very little nutmeg, and *put on the ice until perfectly cold*—this is of the utmost importance. When thoroughly cold, form them into croquettes and roll them in bread-crumbs; beat three eggs (the yolks and whites together), into which dip your croquettes and roll them again in bread-crumbs. Put about two pounds of lard in a frying-pan, and, when very hot, fry your croquettes, which, when a light brown, drain, and serve.

154. **Broiled Lobster.** Take four chicken lobsters (uncooked and perfectly fresh), separate them in two, lengthwise, put a little melted butter upon them, salt, pepper, and some bread-crumbs. Broil them on a gentle fire, and, just before serving, sprinkle over them some chopped parsley. You may serve with them, if desired, a sauce Tartare (Art. 112) or a sauce remoulade (Art. 109).

155. **Deviled Lobster.** Prepare the mixture as described in Art. 153 for lobster croquettes, and mix with it a teaspoonful of mustard. Clean the shells of your lobsters, fill them with the above mixture, which cover lightly with mustard, on top of which sprinkle some bread-crumbs and a very little melted butter. Put them in the oven, and, when colored a light brown, serve.

156. **Lobster à la Bordelaise.** Take the meat of three boiled lobsters, which cut in medium-sized pieces, and put them in a saucepan on the fire for about five minutes, with half a pint of sauce Bordelaise (Art. 101), and serve.

157. **Crawfish à la Bordelaise.** Boil four dozen crawfish as directed in Art. 77, drain, and put them in a saucepan on the fire for about five minutes, with half a pint of sauce Bordelaise (Art. 101), and serve.

158. **Farcied Lobster.** Prepare the mixture as for lobster croquettes (Art. 153), adding a little chopped parsley, and with it fill the shells of two or three lobsters which you have previously washed. Sprinkle some bread-crumbs on top, and a very small quantity of melted butter. Send to the oven, and, when colored a light brown, serve.

159. **Lobster à l'Indienne.** Take two boiled lobsters, divide them in two, and remove the meat from the shells and claws. Wash half a pound of rice, boil it five minutes in boiling water, then put it in cold water for a moment. Drain, and place it in a saucepan with three pints of water, and boil forty minutes. Take half a pint of sauce Veloutée (Art. 82), add your lobsters, place your saucepan at the side of the range so as not to boil, and mix with your sauce a teaspoonful of curry. Drain off your rice, form it in a border on a dish, and place your lobster and sauce in the center.

160. **Fried Frogs' Legs.** Put three dozen frogs' legs in an earthen jar, with salt, thyme, six bay-leaves, three branches of parsley, an onion cut in thin slices, the juice of a lemon, and three or four tablespoonfuls of oil; turn them over on one side, then on the other, several times during an hour; then drain them, dip them in milk, in which you have put a little salt and pepper, roll them in flour, and fry them a light brown, in very hot lard. Serve them with some fried parsley.

161. **Frogs' Legs à la Poulette.** Put three dozen frogs' legs in a saucepan, with an ounce of butter, a claret-glass of white wine, and half a cupful of consommé (stock, [Art. 1](#)), an onion sliced thin, a little thyme, bay-leaf, parsley, a pinch of salt, pepper, and a very little nutmeg. Boil for ten minutes, and then drain. Put a tablespoonful of flour in a saucepan, with an ounce of butter, and mix well together. Strain the liquid in which your frogs' legs were cooked, add to it two yolks of eggs well mixed in about a tablespoonful of water, a tablespoonful of chopped parsley; boil three or four minutes, and serve.

162. **Frogs' Legs à la Marinière.** Put three dozen frogs' legs in a saucepan, with a dozen chopped mushrooms, four shallots also chopped, and two ounces of butter, and toss them on the fire for five or six minutes; then add a tablespoonful of flour, a little salt, pepper, a nutmeg, and moisten with a claret-glass of white wine and a glass of consommé ([Art. 1](#)); boil ten minutes. Mix the yolks of four eggs with two tablespoonfuls of cream, remove your frogs' legs from the fire, and, when boiling has ceased, add your eggs, stirring continually until thoroughly mixed, and serve.

163. **Frogs' Legs à la Maître d'Hôtel.** Boil in water two dozen frogs' legs for about twelve minutes, with a pinch of salt, pepper, and the juice of a lemon. Drain them, and pour over them some melted butter to which you have added the juice of a lemon and a tablespoonful of chopped parsley; serve very hot.

164. **Soft-Shell Crabs.** Take eight soft-shell crabs, remove the gills and the sand. Wash them, then dry them with a cloth, dip them in a little milk, and roll them in flour. Put plenty of lard in a frying-pan, in which, when very hot, fry your crabs. Five minutes will suffice. Serve with them some fried parsley. You may also dip the crabs in beaten eggs, and sprinkle with bread-crumbs before frying.

165. **Farcied Crabs.** Remove the meat from four dozen boiled hard-shelled crabs and chop up fine. Put in a saucepan an onion cut in pieces, and an ounce of butter. When beginning to color slightly, add a dozen chopped mushrooms, a tablespoonful of chopped parsley, and four ounces of bread-crumbs, which you have previously soaked in consommé, and then pressed almost dry; a pinch of salt and pepper, a little cayenne, and half a gill of

tomato sauce (Art. 90). Mix all well together on the fire, and cook for five minutes. Wash your shells and fill them with the foregoing, cover them with bread-crumbs, and a *very little* melted butter on top; send to the oven and color a light brown.

166. **Deviled Crabs.** Proceed as for the foregoing, putting a tablespoonful of mustard in the above mixture, and a layer of mustard on top of each crab before covering with bread-crumbs.

167. **Clam Fritters.** Take fifteen clams, which chop very fine, and put in a bowl with two ounces of flour, two eggs, a pinch of salt and pepper, and a tablespoonful of parsley, which chop fine. Mix all thoroughly together. Put some lard in a frying-pan, into which, when very hot, throw a tablespoonful of your mixture at a time, until you have used the entire quantity; fry on both sides, and serve.

168. **Oyster Fritters.** Prepare as the foregoing.

169. **Fish-Balls.** Wash and peel six potatoes, boil them in a pint of water, with salt, drain them, mash them thoroughly; add an ounce of butter, a pinch of salt and pepper, and an egg; mix all well together, adding six ounces of boiled codfish from which you have removed the bones; mix your fish well with your other ingredients, form into balls about the size of a very small apple, roll them lightly and evenly in flour; fry them on both sides in about half their height of very hot lard, drain off the grease, and serve them very hot.

170. **Codfish au Gratin.** Take two pounds of boiled codfish, from which you have removed the bones, put in a dish with half a pint of béchamel sauce (Art. 83), in which you have mixed four ounces of American cheese. Sprinkle it on top with bread-crumbs and a little melted butter, and send to the oven until colored a bright yellow. Serve. You may, instead of the cheese, mix some chopped mushrooms with your fish. Other boiled fish may be prepared in the same manner.

171. **Snails à la Provençale.** Take four ounces of wood-ashes, which put in a cloth, and tie securely. Then place in a saucepan with about a quart of water, and boil fifteen minutes. Wash well four dozen snails, and put them in your saucepan, and boil them about fifteen minutes. Then take one out,

and try with a larding-needle if you can remove it easily from its shell, and, if so, drain the snails, and take them out of their shells. Put into a saucepan on the fire a tablespoonful of oil, half a dozen mushrooms chopped very fine, some parsley, a clove of garlic, three shallots, all chopped fine, salt, a little red pepper, and a very little nutmeg. Add a tablespoonful of flour, and moisten with three sherry-glasses of white wine, and, as soon as your sauce begins to boil, add your snails, and boil gently for thirty minutes. Your sauce must be thick. Mix the yolks of three eggs in a tablespoonful of milk, and add to your sauce when it has ceased boiling. Put a snail in each shell, and enough sauce to fill each one. Sprinkle bread-crumbs on top, send to the oven for about ten minutes, and serve.

172. **Clams on Toast.** Take fifty clams and roast them very slightly, after which take them out of their shells, chop them fine, and, with all their juice, which you have carefully preserved, put them into a saucepan with a little butter, and stew for a few moments. Just before serving, season them with a little red pepper and a very little Tobasco pepper. First serve to each person a piece of toast, and then the clams to be poured over the toast.

173. **Soft Clams steamed.** Put some boiling water in a saucepan, in the bottom of which lay a brick. Put fifty soft clams in a pan, or in some utensil which may be placed inside your saucepan, and on top of the brick, so that the water shall not touch the clams. Boil quickly about five minutes, covering the saucepan with a lid. Then, if your clams are done, serve them in their shells, with a sauce separately, composed of a little chopped shallot, a little melted butter, salt, pepper, and a little vinegar or the juice of a lemon.

174. **Clams au Gratin.** Prepare exactly as for oysters au gratin (Art. 150).

175. **Mussels à la Marinière.** Take fifty mussels in their shells, remove the black, stringy species of moss attached to them, put them in a covered saucepan on the fire, with about a quarter of a glass of water; toss them for three or four minutes in the saucepan, or until the shells are opened, then drain them, remove one shell of each, leaving the mussel in the other half, and serve them in the following sauce: Chop fine two shallots, which put in a saucepan on the fire, with a tablespoonful of vinegar, reduce one half, and

add a teaspoonful of chervil and tarragon chopped fine; boil for a moment, then add half a pint of sauce Allemande (Art. 81), and a sherry-glass of sherry.

176. **Stewed Terrapin à la Lucie.** Drop three live terrapins into boiling water, and, if large, boil them three hours, or, if moderate sized, two hours and a half. Then pick them, throwing away all of the intestines, heart, head, and most of the feet; also be very particular to cut out the gall, which will be found in the middle of the liver, and throw it away. Scrape out all the fat and meat sticking to the shells, and put into a saucepan with half a pound of *very good* butter, a good deal of salt, and cayenne pepper. Simmer over a slow fire for about two hours. Wine may be added, according to taste, after the terrapin is served.

177. **Stewed Terrapin à la Maryland.** Pick and clean, as the foregoing, two terrapins weighing about six to seven pounds. Boil them in some water with a little salt for about twenty minutes. Drain them, cut them in moderate-sized pieces, and put them in a saucepan with enough cream to cover them, a pinch of salt, pepper, nutmeg, and three wineglasses of sherry. Simmer gently for three quarters of an hour. Mix four yolks of eggs with two tablespoonfuls of cream, add them to your terrapins, and serve very hot.

178. **Stewed Terrapin** (another manner). Prepare your terrapins as the foregoing, add to them half a pint of brandy, touch it with a lighted match, let it burn, and serve.

179. **Glaze.** Put two quarts of consommé (Art. 1 ) in a saucepan on the fire. Reduce it by *very* gentle boiling until it becomes the color of chocolate. Put it in a bowl on the ice, and keep it until needed.

# CHAPTER IV.
# *ENTRÉES.*

## BEEF.

180. **Beef Tongue, Sauce Piquante.** Wash carefully a beef's tongue, boil it an hour, put it in cold water, then remove the skin. Take some strips of larding pork about two inches long, roll them in some parsley chopped very fine, a little pepper and nutmeg, and lard your tongue, which having done, place in a saucepan with a carrot, two onions, six cloves, six pepper-corns, four bay-leaves, and four branches of thyme. Add enough consommé (or stock) to cover the tongue, simmer very gently for four hours, and serve with a sauce piquante (Art. 86 ).

181. **Beef's Tongue à la Jardinière.** Proceed exactly as for the foregoing, and serve on a macédoine of vegetables (Art. 416).

182. **Smoked Beef's Tongue, Wine Sauce with Mushrooms.** Soak a smoked tongue in water the night before it is needed. Then put it in about four quarts of cold water, and boil it slowly about five hours; drain, place it in cold water a moment, remove the skin, trim the thicker end of the tongue neatly, and put it again in hot water for a moment, drain, put it on a dish, pour around it half a pint of Spanish sauce (Art. 80), to which you have added, while on the fire, ten chopped mushrooms and a sherry-glass of sherry.

183. **Hashed Beef.** Take two pounds of cold beef, free from sinew and bone, and chop it up well. Peel and cut in pieces two onions, and put them in a frying-pan with two ounces of butter. When beginning to color very lightly, add your beef, a little salt, pepper, and nutmeg, and a pinch of thyme. Toss all together on the fire ten minutes. Just before serving, sprinkle a tablespoonful of chopped parsley over your hash.

184. **Beef's Brains au Beurre Noir.** Put into cold water three brains, clean them thoroughly, removing all blood, fibers, and pieces of skin, after

which change the water, and let them soak for two hours, being careful to change the water every half-hour. Then put them in a saucepan with six parsley-roots, four cloves, four pepper-corns, an onion cut in pieces, also a carrot, four bay-leaves, four branches of thyme, a teaspoonful of salt, and moisten with a pint of consommé (stock, Art. I) and a claret-glass of white wine. Boil for half an hour, drain, carefully remove all herbs from the brains, and serve with a black-butter sauce.

*Black-Butter Sauce.* Put in a frying-pan four ounces of butter, and when colored black add two tablespoonfuls of vinegar; boil for a moment, add some branches of fried parsley, and serve.

185. **Beef's Brains à la Poulette.** Prepare the brains as the foregoing, and serve with a sauce poulette ([Art. 103](#)).

186. **Palates of Beef, Sauce Robert.** Boil four beef's palates in enough water to cover them, and a little salt, for an hour. Then put them in cold water, and clean them well. Put them in a saucepan with four bay-leaves, four branches of thyme, four cloves, four pepper-corns, four parsley-roots, and half a teaspoonful of salt. Moisten with a pint of consommé (stock, [Art. 1](#)), and simmer them gently for two hours. Then take them from your saucepan, drain them, cut them in squares, and serve them with a sauce Robert ([Art. 92](#)). Other sauces, according to your taste, may be served with this dish.

187. **Ox-Tails braised.** Cut two ox-tails into joints, boil them for half an hour in two quarts of water, and half an ounce of salt; then put them in cold water, drain and place them in a saucepan with a carrot, two onions, six cloves, six pepper-corns, four bay-leaves, four branches of thyme, three branches of parsley, and a little salt; add a quart of consommé (stock, [Art. 1](#)), and simmer gently for five hours; serve with an Italian sauce ([Art. 93](#)).

188. **Beef-Kidneys, Sautés au Vin Blanc.** Cut two beef's kidneys in thin slices; then put in a frying-pan an ounce of butter, into which, when melted, put the kidneys, adding a pinch of salt, the same of pepper, and a very little nutmeg; toss the kidneys in the butter for about five minutes on a good fire; moisten them with one gill of Spanish sauce ([Art. 80](#)), and a sherry-glass of white wine; boil five minutes on the fire, and serve.

189. **Sirloin Steak broiled, with Anchovy Sauce.** Take two and a half pounds of sirloin steak, and put it on a gridiron on a moderate fire, with salt and pepper. Turn the steak often, so that both sides may be equally done; ten minutes should be sufficient to broil it; serve with a white or butter sauce (Art. 14), to which add a teaspoonful of anchovy sauce.

190. **Rump Steak broiled à la Maître d'Hôtel.** Broil as the foregoing; then put two ounces of butter on a very hot plate, so as to melt it completely; add to it a teaspoonful of parsley, which you have previously washed and chopped fine, a pinch of salt and pepper, the juice of a lemon; mix all together, and serve your steak on top.

191. **Porter-house Steak à la Bordelaise.** Broil a porter-house steak as the foregoing, on top of which place small pieces of marrow, cut round, about the size of a fifty-cent piece, and previously boiled; pour around your steak half a pint of sauce Bordelaise (Art. 101). Steak may also be served with a sauce Béarnaise (Art. 88), sauce Hachée (Art. 96), tomato sauce (Art. 90), and others. Potatoes should also be served in whatever manner appropriate to the sauce. Onions cut in slices, rolled in flour and fried in butter a light brown, may also be served on top of a broiled steak.

192. **Tenderloins of Beef, with Potatoes à la Parisienne.** Take three and a half pounds of the fillet of beef, and with a knife remove the skin on top; cut some larding pork into strips, with which lard your beef on the surface. Then in a frying-pan put an onion sliced thin, a branch of thyme, three cloves, three pepper-corns, three bay-leaves, three parsley-roots, and a pinch of salt; moisten with a sherry-glass of white wine and the same of consommé (stock, Art. 1), and place your fillet on top, on which put a few little pieces of butter; simmer gently for about forty minutes, strain the liquid in which your fillet was cooked, pour it over the fillet and serve on a separate dish some potatoes à la Parisienne (Art. 438).

193. **Fillet of Beef Sauté, Madeira Sauce.** Cut eight pieces from a fillet of beef about half an inch thick; put into a saucepan an ounce of butter, a pinch of salt and pepper, a very little nutmeg, and place your pieces of beef on top; toss them for about five minutes on a quick fire, and, when done on both sides, serve them (one piece overlying the other) with half a pint of

Spanish sauce (Art. 80), to which add a wineglass of madeira (or sherry); also serve with this dish some potato croquettes (Art. 423 ).

194. **Braised Beef, Tomato Sauce.** Take three pounds of rump steak; put in a saucepan four ounces of salt pork, which cut in small pieces, place your beef on top, and simmer gently for half an hour, turning it over from time to time; then add as much consommé (stock, Art. 1) as will entirely cover your beef, and two sherry-glasses of white wine, a carrot, an onion, three branches of thyme, three bay-leaves, three cloves, three pepper-corns, three parsley-roots, a pinch of salt and pepper, and a little nutmeg; simmer gently for four hours, drain, and serve with a tomato sauce (Art. 90); or you can serve your beef with the liquid in which it was cooked, after having removed all the grease, and strained carefully.

195. **Beef à la Mode.** Take a round of beef of about four pounds, cut half a pound of larding pork in strips about two inches long, which roll in a tablespoonful of chopped parsley. Make incisions in your beef, and introduce your strips of pork therein. Cut a carrot and an onion in slices, and put them in a saucepan with several branches of parsley, inclosing three cloves, six bay-leaves, three branches of thyme, and tie all together, then add your beef, two claret-glasses of white wine, and a quart of consommé (stock). Simmer gently for three hours, drain off your beef, and strain the liquid in which it was cooked. Then put the beef with its liquid in a saucepan with two carrots and two turnips, which you have previously blanched and cut in slices, and twenty small onions. Simmer gently for an hour and a half, skim off the grease from the liquid, and serve.

196. **Boiled Marrow-Bones.** Tie up in a cloth eight marrow-bones, neatly trimmed, and of about four inches in length, boil an hour, remove the cloth, and serve them on toast, a small napkin neatly arranged around each bone.

197. **Beefsteak Pie.** Take two pounds of cold beef, cut it in small pieces. Put two dozen small white onions, with some butter, in a frying-pan on the fire, and cook gently until browned. Fry half a pound of bacon cut in small pieces, drain, moisten with a pint of Spanish sauce (Art. 80), add your onions, boil for a few moments, add your beef, and put all together in a deep dish, which you have lined with paste, moistening the edges of your

dish so that the paste shall adhere. Cut out some paste the size of your dish and lay it on top. Dip a small brush in beaten egg, with which brush the entire top of your pie, which send to the oven until well colored, and serve. You may mix in your pie, if desired, about twenty-five oysters.

*Paste for the Pie.* Put on a table six ounces of flour, make a hole in the middle, in which place three ounces of butter, and add a claret-glass of water. Mix all well together, and roll it out to the proper thickness.

198. **Broiled Tripe.** Cut some tripe into long pieces, season with pepper and salt. Broil them a nice brown, and serve them on the same plate with an ounce of melted butter, the juice of a lemon well mixed with it, and some chopped parsley. Honeycomb tripe is more delicate than the ordinary tripe.

199. **Tripe à la Lyonnaise.** Cut two pounds of tripe in thin strips, as for Julienne soup, put a sliced onion, with two ounces of butter, in a frying-pan; when well colored, add your tripe, a pinch of salt and pepper, and very little nutmeg. Toss all together until all moisture is absorbed, then add about a quarter of a can of tomatoes, cook for a moment longer, or until very hot, and serve with a little chopped parsley on top.

200. **Fried Tripe.** Cut some tripe in squares. Break two eggs, to which add a little salt and pepper, and beat up your eggs well. Then dip your tripe in the eggs, roll them in flour, fry them in very hot lard, and when they are a light brown drain them, and serve with fried parsley on top.

201. **Tripe à la Mode de Caen.** Put in an earthen pot an onion cut in slices, a carrot in quarters, and four slices of bacon; cover these with a layer of tripe, then a calf's foot cut in four, a pinch of salt and pepper, four cloves, four bay-leaves, three branches of thyme, six pepper-corns, and six parsley-roots. On top of these put a layer of bacon, another of tripe, another calf's foot, cut in pieces, and another layer of tripe, with some bacon on top. Fill your jar three quarters of its height with white wine. Put on the cover, and paste it all around the edge with some flour mixed in a little water, so as to render the jar air-tight. Place it in the oven, and cook for five hours. Instead of white wine, you may substitute cider if you wish.

# VEAL.

202. **Calf's Head en Tortue.** Take a scalded calf's head, put it in a saucepan with enough water to cover it, boil for half an hour, and then plunge it in cold water; mix four tablespoonfuls of flour with a little cold water; cut an onion and a carrot in slices, and put in a saucepan, together with six cloves, six pepper-corns, six parsley-roots, four branches of thyme, six cloves of garlic, six bay-leaves, an ounce of butter, two tablespoonfuls of vinegar, and lastly your calf's head; add enough water to cover it, and boil for two hours. Take half a pint of Spanish sauce (Art. 80), put it on the fire in a saucepan with a wineglass of sherry, about ten mushrooms cut in pieces, and four chickens' livers which you have previously blanched; drain your calf's head and put it on a dish with your sauce; you may also serve with it the brains, from which you have removed all the fibers and loose skin, and also the tongue cut down the middle and the skin taken off.

203. **Calf's Head à la Vinaigrette.** Proceed as for the foregoing, and, just before serving, chop a little parsley, a little chervil, a small onion; add a pinch of salt and pepper, four tablespoonfuls of vinegar and eight tablespoonfuls of oil, and serve with your calf's head.

204. **Baked Calf's Head à l'Italienne.** Boil a calf's head as the preceding, cut it in pieces, which put in a pan, and cover with an Italian sauce (Art. 93 ); sprinkle some bread-crumbs on top, and a very little melted butter; send to the oven, and, when colored a light brown, put it on a dish, and serve with an Italian sauce surrounding it. You may also serve with other sauces, according to your taste.

205. **Calves' Tongues.** Take four calves' tongues, which prepare as beef's tongue (Art. 180), and, after cooking two hours, take them off the fire, remove all skin, and cut them through the middle of the tongue. Put them on a dish, and serve with them an Italian sauce (Art. 93), sauce poivrade (Art. 95 ), tomato sauce (Art. 90), or with a macédoine of vegetables (Art. 416).

206. **Calves' Brains au Gratin.** Put into cold water four calves' brains, clean them thoroughly, removing all blood, fibers, and pieces of skin, after which change the water and let them soak for two hours, being careful to change the water every half-hour, then drain them; put for a moment in a saucepan on the fire, four ounces of butter and a large sliced onion; add the

brains, season with pepper and salt, and let them simmer gently, turning them over so that both sides may be done, and drain off the grease; butter a deep dish, which sprinkle all over with bread-crumbs; add a *very* thick béchamel sauce (Art. 83) to the brains, which put in the dish, let them cool, sprinkle bread-crumbs and some melted butter on top; send to a moderate oven for half an hour, and serve.

207. **Calves' Brains à la Poulette.** Proceed as for beef's brain, allowing only half the time to boil; put four brains on a dish, and pour over them a sauce à la poulette (Art. 103).

208. **Fried Calves' Brains, Tomato Sauce.** Boil four calves' brains as the preceding, drain them, and cut them into medium-sized pieces; beat up two eggs, to which add a little salt and pepper; dip the brains in the eggs and then sprinkle them with bread-crumbs; put plenty of lard in a frying-pan, and, when very hot, fry the brains, and also some parsley; drain, and serve with a tomato sauce in a separate dish.

209. **Calves' Ears farcied.** Take four well-scalded calves' ears; put them in two quarts of boiling water on the fire for half an hour, after which put in cold water; then clean the inside of the ears well, and place in a saucepan with a quart of consommé (Art. 1), a claret-glass of white wine, the juice of a lemon, four cloves, four branches of thyme, three bay-leaves, one clove of garlic, and a dozen branches of parsley tied together; boil gently for two hours, drain them, and fill the inside of the ears with a chicken farce (Art. 11), to which add a tablespoonful of parsley chopped fine; sprinkle with bread-crumbs and a few drops of melted butter; send them to the oven, and, when a nice light brown, serve with a tomato sauce (Art. 90) surrounding them, or a sauce piquante (Art. 86).

210. **Calves' Liver Sauté, Sauce Poivrade.** Cut two pounds of calf's liver in equal pieces, put two ounces of melted butter in a frying-pan with your calf's liver, fry on both sides, and serve with a sauce poivrade (Art. 95).

211. **Broiled Calf's Liver.** Cut thin two pounds of calf's liver in equal pieces, roll in flour, and broil on a gridiron; a little melted butter on each piece; broil on both sides and put them on a dish, with a little melted butter,

a little chopped parsley, the juice of a lemon, salt, and pepper, well mixed together.

212. **Calf's Liver with Bacon.** Fry two pounds of calf's liver, cut in pieces, and serve with very thin slices of bacon, or with half a pint of Spanish sauce (Art. 80), to which add a claret-glass of port or claret, and three tablespoonfuls of currant jelly mixed in a tablespoonful of water. Boil gently for three or four minutes, and serve.

213. **Braised Calf's Liver à la Bourgignone.** Take an entire calf's liver, lard it thickly with larding pork, and put it in a saucepan with an ounce of butter, four bay-leaves, three branches of thyme, three cloves, a sliced onion and carrot; cook for ten minutes, moisten with a pint of Spanish sauce (Art. 80) and a claret-glass of red wine. Simmer gently for an hour and a half, and take out your calf's liver, which keep very hot. Remove all grease from the liquid in which it was cooked, strain it, pour it over the liver, which should be left whole, and serve.

214. **Calf's Heart aux Fines Herbes.** Cut three calves' hearts in round or oval pieces, put them in a frying-pan in which you have melted an ounce and a half of butter, and, adding a little salt and pepper, cook gently, taking care to turn over until they are a good color on both sides, then drain them, leaving the butter in your pan, into which throw three chopped shallots. Toss them for half a minute in your butter, which pour over your calf's heart, and, when serving, put a tablespoonful of chopped parsley on top.

215. **Calf's Feet à la Poulette.** Prepare four calf's feet as the foregoing, cooking half an hour longer; drain them, cut them in pieces, and serve with a sauce à la poulette (Art. 103).

216. **Veal Pot-Pie.** Cut two pounds of a shoulder of veal in medium-sized pieces, which boil in a quart of water ten minutes, then put them for a moment in cold water, drain them, and place them in a saucepan on the fire with a quart of water, some salt, white pepper, a little nutmeg, and several branches of parsley, inclosing three bay-leaves, three branches of thyme, four pepper-corns, tied all together. Boil an hour. Mix in a bowl three tablespoonfuls of flour with half a glass of water, which add to your veal and boil ten minutes longer. Put in a bowl four ounces of flour with a teaspoonful of Royal Baking Powder, and mix well with a little water, so as

to form a soft paste, with which make little round balls, poach them in boiling water, add them to your veal in the saucepan, having removed the parsley with its seasoning, and serve.

217. **Sweetbreads aux Fines Herbes.** Take some sweetbreads (in quantity according to their size), put them in a saucepan with some water, and simmer them gently for about ten minutes. Drain them, remove from them all skin and fat, shape them in round pieces, and put them in a frying-pan in which you have melted an ounce of butter and added a little salt and pepper. Let them simmer gently, turning them over now and then, and when they are a good color take them out. Chop three shallots and six mushrooms, put them in the butter in which your sweetbreads were cooked, let them remain on the fire for about two minutes, adding a little chopped parsley and the juice of a lemon, which pour over your sweetbreads, and serve. You can also prepare sweetbreads in the same manner, and serve with a tomato sauce (Art. 90), Spanish sauce (Art. 80), or stewed with sauce à la poulette (Art. 103 ), with a tablespoonful of chopped parsley added, or sauce Béarnaise (Art. 88).

218. **Sweetbreads larded with Peas.** Blanch some sweetbreads as the foregoing, pare them neatly, and lard them thickly with larding pork. Put in a pan very thin slices of ham, a carrot, an onion cut in thin slices, two cloves, two bay-leaves, a clove of garlic, two branches of thyme, and place the sweetbreads on top. Cover them about three quarters with consommé (stock, Art. 1), put them in the oven, and baste them from time to time with the liquid in the pan, and, when well colored, take them from the oven and serve them on top of about a quart of peas, previously boiled, a little butter, salt, pepper, and a little sugar added to them.

219. **Sweetbread Croquettes.** Boil four sweetbreads, and let them become cold; then chop them very fine, add about ten mushrooms and some truffles also chopped fine. Take about half a pint of Allemande sauce (Art. 81), mix well with your sweetbreads, which put on the ice to become thoroughly cold; form the mixture into croquettes, dip them in two beaten eggs, roll them in bread-crumbs; fry them a bright yellow in very hot lard, drain them, and serve them with fried parsley or with green peas.

220. **Veal Cutlets à l'Allemande.** Take three pounds of veal cutlets, which cut in round pieces; break two eggs in a bowl, adding some salt and pepper and an ounce of melted butter; beat all well together, and dip into it your veal cutlets, after which sprinkle some bread-crumbs over them. Then put them on a moderate fire, in a frying-pan, in which you have melted two ounces of butter, and, when they are fried a light brown on both sides, serve with half a pint of tomato sauce (Art. 90).

221. **Veal Chops à la Mayonnaise.** Put eight veal chops in a flat saucepan, moisten them with their height of consommé (Art. 1), add a little salt, pepper, nutmeg, and simmer gently for an hour, after which take them out and put them on the ice until very cold; serve them in a circle with whatever jelly remains, and in the center a sauce Mayonnaise (Art. 113), or a sauce ravigote cold (Art. 112).

222. **Veal Chops Piqués.** Take eight veal chops, make six incisions in each, in which insert three pieces of truffles cut square at one end and pointed at the other, and three small pieces of boiled ham cut in the same manner; put in a flat saucepan an onion and a carrot cut in slices, a thin slice of ham, three cloves, three pepper-corns, three bay-leaves, three branches of parsley, the same of thyme, two cloves of garlic, and a pinch of salt and pepper. Place your chops on top and moisten them with three quarters of their height of consommé (Art. 1) and a claret-glass of white wine. Send them to the oven for an hour, baste them every ten minutes with their liquor, and serve them with a sauce financière, made in the following manner: Put in a saucepan half a pint of Spanish sauce (Art. 80), to which add a wineglass of sherry, a few truffles cut in quarters, also olives from which you have removed the stones, a few pieces of sweet-bread blanched and boiled, and a few chickens' livers blanched, boiled, and cut in quarters.

223. **Braised Tendons of Veal a la Macédoine.** Cut your tendons of veal three inches in length and one inch thick, put them in a pan with two slices of ham, a carrot and an onion cut in thin slices, two cloves, two bay-leaves, two branches of thyme, and a clove of garlic; cover them about three quarters with consommé (stock, Art. 1), and put them in the oven, basting them from time to time with the liquid in the pan. Take half a pint of Spanish sauce (Art. 80), to which add a pinch of sugar, and, when your

sauce is boiling, add a quart of macédoine (Art. 416), which put on a dish, your tendons of veal on top, and serve.

224. **Braised Tendons of Veal with Purée of Celery.** Braise your tendons as the foregoing; then put them on a dish and cover them with a *very thick* sauce Allemande (Art. 81); let them become cold, and, when the sauce is firmly set, beat up two eggs, adding a little salt and pepper, in which dip your tendons, and then sprinkle them with bread-crumbs. Put in a frying-pan about two pounds of lard, in which, when very hot, fry your tendons. Serve them in the form of a circle, one piece overlapping the other, and a purée of celery (Art. 392) in the center. You may also serve with a sauce suprême (Art. 99) around the tendons.

225. **Fricandeau of Veal.** Take three pounds from the tenderest part of the thigh, about two inches in thickness; lard it well on the surface, put it in a saucepan with same ingredients as for braised tendons of veal (Art. 223), moisten with enough consommé (stock, Art. 1) to reach the surface of your veal. Put on the fire until boiling, then send to the oven, basting it frequently with its liquor. Let it remain in the oven three hours, and serve it with either the liquid in which it was cooked, after having strained it and removed all grease, or on a purée of peas (Art. 446), or a purée of sorrel (469).

226. **Blanquette of Veal.** Take three pounds of a shoulder of veal, cut it in pieces, which put in a saucepan with three pints of water, a pinch of salt, several branches of parsley, inclosing three cloves, three pepper-corns, three bay-leaves, three branches of thyme, two cloves of garlic, and tie all together. When commencing to boil, skim thoroughly, and then boil an hour and a half. Put half a pint of sauce Allemande (Art. 80) on the fire, but do not allow it to boil; chop a dozen mushrooms, add them to your sauce, drain off your veal, and serve together with your sauce.

227. **Minced Veal, with Poached Eggs on Top.** Chop fine two pounds of cold veal, from which you have removed the sinews, and add a little more than half a pint of sauce béchamel (Art. 83), a little salt, pepper, and nutmeg, and an ounce of butter; put all together in a saucepan on the fire for a few moments, remove it from the fire, and place it on a dish with ten poached eggs on top. Minced chicken is prepared in exactly the same manner.

228. **Veal Kidneys Sautés.** Take three veal kidneys, which cut very thin, and proceed as for beef kidneys (Art. 188).

229. **Deviled Veal Kidneys.** Take three veal kidneys, which separate in two, lengthwise; then from the flat side remove all fibrous particles from the inside; cover them on both sides with mustard, and add a little red pepper; roll them well in bread-crumbs, put a little melted butter on both sides; broil on a gentle fire. Mutton, beef, and pork kidneys are treated in the same manner, except that they are cut in quarters instead of in halves.

## MUTTON.

230. **Sheep's Brains.** Prepare and cook the brains as for calf's brains (Art. 208).

231. **Sheep's Kidneys en Brochette.** Take ten sheep's kidneys, remove all the skin which covers them, split them without cutting the sinew, pass a skewer through them, sprinkle a pinch of salt and pepper over them, and broil them on a good fire, taking care to turn them so as to broil on both sides; after which remove the skewer. Put two ounces of melted butter on a dish, a tablespoonful of chopped parsley, the juice of a lemon, mix all well together, and serve.

232. **Mutton Chops à la Soubise.** Take ten rib chops, season with pepper and salt, dip them in two ounces of melted butter, and cover them thickly with bread-crumbs; broil them, and, when they are well colored, serve them on a dish, with a sauce soubise (Art. 94). You may also serve them with a sauce Robert (Art. 92), or a tomato sauce (Art. 90), or with a macédoine (Art. 416) in the center.

233. **Mutton Chops Sautés.** Take ten mutton chops, which put in a frying-pan in which you have melted two ounces of butter; sprinkle them with a little salt and pepper, and cook them on a quick fire; four or five minutes will be sufficient. Serve with purée of turnips (Art. 398).

234. **Mutton Chops à la Pompadour.** Take ten mutton chops, which cook as described in mutton chops sautés (Art. 233); then let them become cold; peel and chop ten onions, which put in a saucepan with two ounces of butter. When colored lightly, add two tablespoonfuls of flour, a pinch of salt and pepper, and a very little nutmeg. Mix all well together and add about two sherry-glasses of cream. Reduce for about fifteen minutes, and then allow your mixture to become cold, then cover each chop with it on both sides; beat up four eggs, into which dip the chops and cover with bread-crumbs; again dip them in egg, and again cover with bread-crumbs and a few drops of melted butter. Send them to the oven, and, when a bright yellow color, serve them with a purée of French chestnuts (Art. 442) in the center.

235. **Mutton Chops en Crépinette.** Put eight mutton chops in a frying-pan in which you have melted an ounce of butter, adding a pinch of salt, pepper, and nutmeg; when the chops are colored on both sides, take them out and let them become cold. Chop fine three quarters of a pound of sausage-meat, add eight mushrooms, a little parsley and sage, all chopped fine; mix all together, and cover your chops on both sides with the farce, and wrap up each chop with the caul of pork. Send them to a gentle oven on a buttered pan, and, when well colored, serve with a tomato sauce (Art. 90), sauce piquante (Art. 86), or sauce ravigote hot (Art. 111).

236. **Breast of Mutton.** Take two breasts of mutton, which put in a saucepan with a quart of consommé (stock, Art. 1) and a quart of water, an onion and a carrot cut in slices, three bay-leaves, four cloves, three branches of thyme, two cloves of garlic, and four parsley-roots, and boil gently for two hours; then drain them and put them between two dishes, with a weight on top to flatten them; when cold, cut them oval, dip them in two beaten eggs to which you have added an ounce of melted butter and a pinch of salt and pepper. Sprinkle them thickly with bread-crumbs and a few drops of melted butter, and send to the oven; when well colored, serve with a sauce piquante (Art. 86).

237. **Sheep's Feet à la Poulette.** Split in halves a dozen scalded sheep's feet, and proceed as for calf's feet à la poulette (Art. 215); serve very hot.

238. **Roast Leg of Mutton à la Bretonne.** Take a leg of mutton of about six or seven pounds; put it to roast, taking care to baste it from time to time; an hour and a quarter is sufficient to roast it. Put in the oven six onions without being peeled, and, as soon as they are done, peel them and put them in a saucepan, with a pinch of salt, pepper, and nutmeg; add to them half a pint of Spanish sauce (Art. 80 ), which reduce fifteen minutes, strain, and serve with your mutton.

239. **Boiled Leg of Mutton.** Take a leg of mutton of about six pounds and place in a saucepan with a sliced onion, a carrot, three bay-leaves, three cloves of garlic, three branches of thyme, four cloves, six parsley-roots, an ounce of salt, and enough water to cover them. Boil for an hour and a half, and serve with a sauce béchamel (Art. 83), to which add some chopped parsley or capers.

240. **Roast Saddle of Mutton.** Take a medium-sized saddle of mutton, cut the flaps square and roll them up, tie some twine around the saddle, so as to give it a neat shape, season with salt and pepper, and roast it for three quarters of an hour; remove your twine, and serve with some currant jelly.

241. **Leg of Mutton en Venaison.** Take a medium-sized leg of mutton, from which cut the knuckle-bone at the second joint and put it in an earthen jar with two sliced onions, a carrot, six bay-leaves, six cloves of garlic, ten cloves, ten pepper-corns, six branches of thyme, six parsley-roots, a teaspoonful of pepper, and a pint of vinegar. Let your mutton remain in these ingredients three days, and stir every six hours; then take it out of the earthen jar, roast it, and serve with a sauce poivrade (Art. 95).

242. **Irish Stew.** Take four pounds from a breast of mutton, take off the skin and the fat, cut it in medium-sized pieces, which put in a saucepan with three pints of water, half an ounce of salt, a pinch of pepper, and a very little nutmeg. When beginning to boil, skim all the grease off carefully, add two carrots and two turnips cut in slices, six medium-sized onions peeled, and some branches of parsley, inclosing three cloves, one clove of garlic, six pepper-corns, two bay-leaves, two branches of thyme, and tie all together. Boil an hour and a half. Peel and cut in pieces eight potatoes, boil them, and

add them to your stew. Mix two ounces of flour in a little water, making a smooth, soft paste, and pour it over your stew, stirring constantly. Boil ten minutes, remove the bunch of parsley, and serve. You may put a tablespoonful of chopped parsley over your stew if desired.

243. **Shoulder of Mutton farcied.** Bone a shoulder of mutton, take out a portion of the meat without breaking the skin, remove the sinews and chop the meat with half of its weight of fat salt pork, and an ounce of ham; when chopped very fine, add a medium-sized onion also chopped fine, and four ounces of bread-crumbs which you have soaked in consommé (Art. 1) and then pressed almost dry, an egg, and a pinch of salt, pepper, and a very little nutmeg. Mix all well together, and place this farce in the inside of your shoulder. Roll up and sew together with a larding-needle; then put it in a saucepan with a sliced onion and carrot, two bay-leaves, two branches of thyme, one clove of garlic, three cloves, and three pepper-corns. Moisten three quarters of its height with consommé (stock, Art. 1) and a claret-glass of white wine. Put it in the oven for two hours, basting it from time to time with its liquor. Drain your shoulder of mutton, reduce its liquor one half, skim off the grease, and serve it on the same dish with the mutton. You may serve with this a purée of turnips (Art. 398), purée of peas (Art. 446), or various other vegetables.

244. **Epigramme of Lamb.** Put a breast of spring lamb in a saucepan with enough consommé (Art. 1) to cover it. Boil gently for an hour and a half; place it between two dishes, with a weight on top; when cold, cut it in the shape of chops and dip in two beaten eggs, to which you have added a little salt and pepper; then roll them in bread-crumbs and send them to the oven in a pan, with a little melted butter on top. Put eight lamb chops in a saucepan with half an ounce of butter, a little salt and pepper; color them on both sides. Remove your breast of lamb from the oven, and serve together with the chops, in a circle, first a breast of lamb and then a chop, and some asparagus ends or macédoine (Art. 416) in the center.

245. **Breast of Lamb, with Asparagus.** Prepare two breasts of spring lamb as the foregoing, serve them in a circle on a dish, with a garnish of green asparagus ends in the center; then take the green ends of about two bunches of asparagus, boil them very tender, adding a little salt; drain them,

and add them to half a pint of very hot Allemande sauce (Art. 81), a pinch of sugar, and nutmeg, which pour around your breasts of lamb, and serve.

# PORK.

246. **Pig's Tongue.** Prepare and cook as for calf's tongue (Art. 205), and serve with a sauce piquante (Art. 86), or sauce ravigote (Art. 110), or sauce tartare (Art. 112).

247. **Fillet of Pork à la Fermière.** Take five small fillets of pork, divide them in two, shaping them alike, and put them in an earthen jar; peel and slice a carrot and an onion, put them in a frying-pan with a claret-glass of white wine, a clove of garlic, two bay-leaves, two branches of thyme, two cloves, four parsley-roots, a little mace, and a pinch of pepper. Boil them for five minutes, let them become cold, pour over your fillets of pork, and allow them to soak twelve hours; then drain off your fillets and put them in a saucepan with three quarters of their height of consommé (stock, Art. 1) and three tablespoonfuls of the liquid in which your fillets were soaked. Boil on a good fire for half an hour, drain them, keep them hot, reduce the liquid one half in which they were cooked, drain it, and serve with your fillets.

248. **Boiled Pigs' Feet.** Take eight pigs' feet, and, if raw, tie them securely in a cloth so as to preserve their shape, put them in a saucepan with half an ounce of salt, three cloves, three pepper-corns, three branches of thyme, three bay-leaves, a little mace, two parsley-roots, a sliced carrot, a wineglass of vinegar, and moisten liberally with water. Simmer gently for six hours, let them become cold in their liquor; remove the cloths in which they were tied, dip them in beaten egg, roll them thickly in bread-crumbs, broil them, and, when a deep yellow color, serve very hot. You may serve with them a sauce piquante (Art. 86).

249. **Pigs' Kidneys Sautés.** Chop two shallots and a small onion very fine, put them in a frying-pan with an ounce of butter, color them very gently, and add four pigs' kidneys cut in thin slices, a pinch of salt and pepper, and a little nutmeg; toss them for a few minutes without stopping, and, when they are almost done, add a teaspoonful of flour, which mix well with the kidneys, a sherry-glass of white wine, a tablespoonful of chopped

parsley; mix all well together, and serve, without having allowed them to boil.

250. **Sausage of Fresh Pork.** Take a pound of lean pork and the same of fat pork; chop them very fine, adding half an ounce of salt, a pinch of pepper, a little nutmeg, a pinch of sage, a shallot and a teaspoonful of parsley, both chopped fine; mix all well together, and put this farce in the thin skin used for enveloping sausages, by means of a funnel; tie all together securely in several places, and broil them a fine light color, and serve. Flat sausages are prepared in the same manner.

251. **Spare-Ribs, Apple Sauce.** Take eight ribs of fresh pork, put them in a pan, with a pinch of salt sprinkled on top, and some melted butter; send to the oven for an hour, or until well colored. Pare a dozen apples, put them in a saucepan with two ounces of sugar, a little nutmeg, a *very* little cinnamon, the juice of a lemon, and a little water. Put your apples through a sieve, and serve, when very cold, with your roast.

252. **Pork Chops, Sauce Robert.** Take eight pork chops, put them in a frying-pan in which you have melted an ounce of butter, sprinkle them with a little salt and pepper, a very little nutmeg, a pinch of allspice, and color them on both sides on a quick fire; serve them on a dish with a sauce Robert (Art. 92 ), Italian sauce (Art. 93), sauce ravigote hot (Art. 110 ), sauce piquante (Art. 86), or tomato sauce (Art. 90 ).

253. **Broiled Pork Chops.** Proceed as for broiled mutton chops (Art. 232), and serve with any of the above sauces.

254. **Pork Chops à l'Indienne.** Fry as for pork chops, sauce Robert (Art. 252), and drain off the grease. In a saucepan put half a pint of Spanish sauce (Art. 80) and a teaspoonful of curry; add your chops, simmer gently for about ten minutes, and serve them with the sauce around them, and boiled rice in the center.

255. **Pig's Head, Sauce Poivrade.** Cut the meat from a pig's head, divide in pieces of about two inches long, put them in an earthen jar with an onion cut in slices, three bay-leaves, three branches of thyme, three cloves, three pepper-corns, a pinch of pepper, two parsley-roots, two claret-glasses of vinegar, and soak twenty-four hours; then put them in a saucepan with

enough water to cover them, a carrot and an onion cut in slices. Boil gently two hours, drain your pork, and serve with a sauce poivrade (Art. 95).

256. **Frankfort Sausages, with Sourcrout.** Take ten Frankfort sausages, boil them five minutes in boiling water, and serve them with a garnish of sourcrout (Art. 417).

257. **Roast Sucking Pig farcied.** Take a sucking pig, make an incision in the top of the thighs and shoulders; remove all sinews from the intestines, which chop fine with a pound of bread-crumbs which you have soaked in water and then pressed almost dry. Put two sliced onions in a saucepan on the fire, with an ounce of butter, for five minutes; then add your mixture, half an ounce of salt, a good pinch of pepper, a little nutmeg, a pinch of allspice, three times as much of sage; mix all well together, and with this mixture stuff the inside of the pig and sew up the paunch. Put it on a pan to roast for four hours, with a claret-glass of white wine. Baste it several times just before serving, remove the string with which it was sewed, strain, remove all grease from its liquor, and serve with the pig.

258. **Glazed Ham.** Trim a ham of about five pounds, cut the thigh-bone, and put it in cold water to soak, if old, twenty-four hours, during which time change the water twice; if new, twelve hours will suffice. After soaking, wrap it up in a cloth and put it in a large pot, with enough water to cover it; add a carrot, an onion, three bay-leaves, three cloves, one clove of garlic, six pepper-corns, and simmer very gently five hours; after which remove the pot from the fire, and a moment afterward take out your ham; unfasten the cloth, remove the thigh-bone, leaving the knuckle-bone. Drain your ham, put it back again in the cloth in a deep, round bowl, with a weight on top, until the next day, then take off the cloth, trim the ham carefully, and remove the rind within five inches of the knuckle-bone; cut it in points, brush the ham over with glaze (Art. 179). Decorate with aspic jelly (Art. 278 or 279); garnish the knuckle-bone with a ruffle of paper, and serve.

259. **Glazed Ham with Champagne Sauce.** Proceed as for the foregoing, put half a pint of Spanish sauce (Art. 80) in a saucepan on the fire, add a glass of champagne or champagne cider, boil for a moment, and serve in a sauce-boat with your ham.

260. **Glazed Ham with Truffles.** Proceed as for glazed ham ([Art. 258](#)), except that instead of boiling five hours, boil four hours. Then take out a quart of its liquid and substitute a bottle of white wine. Simmer slowly for an hour, drain, then remove the napkin, take out the thigh-bone, leaving the knuckle-bone joint. Cover the back of the ham with incisions, in which insert large slices of truffles, which you have previously cooked in a little of the ham's liquor, some of which now pour over the ham. Wrap it up again very tight in the napkin, and finish as for glazed ham.

261. **Ham à l'Américaine.** Take a ham of about five pounds, prepare as for glazed ham, put it in a pot with a quart of claret, and enough water to cover it. Simmer very gently five hours. Then take it out, sprinkle lightly with sugar, send to the oven, and, when well-colored, serve with a garnish of spinach, Brussels sprouts, green peas, or other green vegetables, according to taste.

262. **Ham à la Zingara.** Cut ten slices of raw ham rather thick, put them in a frying-pan, in which you have melted a little lard. Color them on both sides, take them out of your frying-pan and keep them hot. Mix with your lard two ounces of bread-crumbs, press through a sieve, and put them on the fire five minutes, stirring constantly; moisten with a sherry-glass of white wine; add a little salt, pepper, and nutmeg, and a little chopped parsley. Mix all well together, and serve with your slices of ham on top.

263. **Roast Ham.** Trim and pare a ham, of about five pounds, soak it for two days, changing the water about every eight hours, after which let it soak for about half a day in two bottles of white wine; then put it to roast by a slow fire, for about four hours, covering it underneath with thin pieces of larding pork, and basting it often with hot water, which you have put in your pan. When your ham is nearly done, take off the rind within six inches of the knuckle-bone, cut it in long points; sprinkle the ham on top with bread-crumbs, and serve with a hunter sauce ([Art. 97](#)).

264. **Ham Toast.** Cut the crust from eight slices of bread of medium thickness, spread some butter thickly on top, and a little mustard, then some grated cheese and ham, very little chopped shallot, and some cayenne pepper. Send to the oven for a few moments, or until the cheese is dissolved, and serve immediately.

# POULTRY AND GAME, WITH ROASTS OF SAME.

265. **Broiled Chicken.** Take four spring chickens, put some alcohol on a plate, light it, and pass your chickens over the flame, to singe off any hair which may remain. Split them in two, clean them, wash them well, and dry with a cloth, flatten them with a cleaver; broil them on a moderate fire, and, when well colored on both sides, serve them on a very hot dish, on which you have put an ounce of butter, a pinch of salt and pepper, the juice of a lemon, a tablespoonful of chopped parsley, and mix all well together. Serve some water-cresses around them.

266. **Broiled Chickens (Deviled).** Take three medium-sized spring chickens, prepare them as the foregoing, spread them lightly with a layer of mustard, sprinkle them with bread-crumbs, and broil them on a very gentle fire. To be certain that they are thoroughly done, lift up the thigh, and if not red underneath, they are sufficiently cooked. Serve very hot.

267. **Roast Spring Chickens.** Clean three or four spring chickens, truss them, put them to roast, sprinkle them with a pinch of salt, and a very little melted butter, with which baste them from time to time. From thirty to thirty-five minutes should be sufficient to roast them. When they are a fine color, remove your skewers, and take a gill of consommé (Art. 1), reduce it on the fire one half, mix it with the drippings of your chicken, strain, pour it over them, and serve with water-cresses around them.

268. **Fricassée of Chicken.** Clean and wash two chickens, cut off the thighs, legs, wings, and breasts, which put in a saucepan with a quart of water, and blanch them ten minutes; then put them in cold water for a moment; after which place them in a saucepan with a pint of consommé (Art. 1), a pint of water, several branches of parsley, inclosing four cloves, four pepper-corns, three branches of thyme, three bay-leaves, and tie all together, add one half ounce of salt, two pinches of pepper, and a little nutmeg. Simmer gently forty minutes. Put in another saucepan two ounces of butter, and the same of flour, mix well together, then add little by little three quarters of a pint of the liquid in which your chickens were cooked, and which you have strained. Boil gently. Take the yolks of four eggs, the juice of a lemon, and a tablespoonful of water. Remove your sauce from the fire, and, when it has ceased boiling, add your eggs, stirring until well

mixed. Put your chickens on a dish, pour the sauce over them, and serve. You may add mushrooms to your sauce, green peas, or the green ends of asparagus.

269. **Chicken à la Marengo.** Prepare and cut up two chickens as the foregoing, put them in a frying-pan with two tablespoonfuls of oil, color your chickens a light brown, then remove them from the frying-pan and put them in a saucepan with a half pint of Spanish sauce (Art. 80), six tablespoonfuls of tomatoes, a claret-glass of white wine, a pinch of salt and pepper, a little nutmeg, and boil for thirty minutes on a good fire; add a dozen mushrooms, the same of truffles cut in quarters, and serve. You may also serve, around your chicken, eggs fried in oil and small pieces of bread fried in butter.

270. **Chicken Sauté à la Hongroise.** Clean and cut up two chickens as for fricassée, and put them in a saucepan with two ounces of butter and two onions cut in small pieces. When beginning to color, add two ounces of flour, which mix well with your other ingredients; moisten with a pint of milk, add a little salt, pepper, and nutmeg, several branches of parsley, inclosing two cloves, two pepper-corns, two bay-leaves, two branches of thyme, and tie all together. Boil very gently, skim off the grease, remove your parsley with its spices, and serve.

271. **Chicken Sauté aux Fines Herbes.** Clean and cut in pieces two young chickens, and put them in a saucepan, with four chopped shallots and two ounces of butter. Turn your chicken continually, so as not to stick to the pan, add a little salt, pepper, and nutmeg, and half a pint of Spanish sauce (Art. 80). Chop a dozen mushrooms very fine, boil five minutes longer, and, just before serving, add a tablespoonful of chopped parsley, which mix with your sauce, and serve very hot.

272. **Chicken à la Financière.** Prepare two young chickens as for a fricassée, put them in a frying-pan with an ounce of butter. When beginning to color, remove them from the frying-pan and place them in a saucepan with half a pint of Spanish sauce (Art. 80), two wineglasses of sherry, a pinch of pepper, salt, and nutmeg, several branches of parsley, inclosing two cloves, a little thyme, and two bay-leaves, and tie all together. Boil for about thirty-five minutes. Cut in pieces six truffles, six mushrooms, a

sweet-bread tossed in a little butter, a dozen chickens' kidneys, let the sauce boil up again, and serve.

273. **Suprême de Volaille.** Take four very tender chickens, cut the skin which covers the breast, so as to remove the fillets. Pass the point of a knife between the breast-bone and the fillet as far as the wish-bone, then remove the fillet entire, without tearing it, and proceed the same with the other fillets. Place them on a table, and open them carefully, dividing the large fillets from the small ones (those underneath), but not separating them, and introduce between each fillet a tablespoonful of chicken farce (Art. 11), with which you have mixed three truffles chopped very fine; make three or four incisions on the top of each fillet, moisten lightly with a little white of egg, decorate the top with thin slices of truffles cut in the form of small cockscombs; again moisten lightly with white of egg, place the fillets in a saucepan, adding a wineglass of sherry, half an ounce of butter, three sherry-glasses of consommé (Art. 1), put the lid on your saucepan, and boil gently ten minutes. Serve them in half a pint of sauce suprême (Art. 99), to which you have added about eight chopped truffles.

274. **Chicken à la Toulouse.** Take the eight thighs of the foregoing, and put them in a saucepan with some consommé (Art. 1), several branches of parsley, inclosing two bay-leaves, two branches of thyme, two cloves, two pepper-corns, and tie all together; also, add an onion and a carrot, cut in slices; boil gently for about forty minutes, and, if sufficiently done, drain them, place them in a circle on a dish, and serve them with a sauce Allemande (Art. 81) in the center, to which you have added a dozen chopped mushrooms.

275. **Chicken with Rice.** Clean and prepare two chickens, put them in a saucepan with enough consommé (Art. 1) to cover them. After boiling forty minutes, drain them. Wash half a pound of rice and boil it for ten minutes, put it in cold water, drain it and moisten with a quarter of the liquid in which the chickens were cooked and which you have strained, add a pinch of salt, pepper, and nutmeg. Simmer gently for forty minutes, add an ounce of butter to your rice, mix all well together, place on a dish, and serve your chickens cut up in pieces on top.

276. **Chicken Sauté au Chasseur.** Clean and prepare two chickens, cut up in pieces. Cut half a pound of bacon in small pieces, and put on the fire, in a saucepan, for about five minutes; add your chicken, and, when colored on one side, turn over on the other. When done, pour off all the grease in your saucepan, moisten your chicken with half a pint of Spanish sauce (Art. 80) and a claret-glass of white wine. Peel two dozen little onions, put them in a frying-pan with a little lard, and, when colored, add them to your chicken a moment before serving, with a pinch of pepper, salt, nutmeg, and a dozen mushrooms cut in quarters. Remove all grease from your sauce, and serve.

277. **Boiled Fowl, Caper Sauce.** Prepare and clean a fowl, pass a wooden skewer through the thighs, put it in a saucepan with half a pound of salt pork, and enough water to cover the chicken. Boil for an hour and a half, drain, put it on a dish, and pour over it half a pint of white sauce (Art. 84), to which you have added a handful of capers. Instead of capers you may add a tablespoonful of chopped parsley, or two dozen oysters, blanched and drained.

278. **Aspic de Foie Gras.** Heat three pints of consommé (Art. 1), to which add three ounces of gelatine, a branch of tarragon, a tablespoonful of tarragon vinegar, and two wineglasses of madeira (or sherry). Simmer gently, and, when your gelatine is dissolved, remove your saucepan to the side of the range. Mix the whites of four eggs with a glass of cold water, and add them to your jelly, also the juice of a lemon; stir until thoroughly mixed. Simmer gently at the side of the range for half an hour, then strain through a flannel several times, or until perfectly clear. Take a round mold with a hole in the middle, place it on the top of some cracked ice, and pour in the bottom a few tablespoonfuls of jelly. When stiff, decorate it with truffles and the whites of hard-boiled eggs, cut in any fancy form which pleases you, then put on top another layer of jelly, let it stiffen, then add a layer of pâté de foie gras cut in pieces, then another layer of jelly, and so on, in the same manner, until your mold is filled, then put it on the ice for an hour. Then turn out your jelly on a dish, and put in the middle a sauce remoulade (cold, Art. 109), or sauce ravigote (cold, Art. 112), or sauce tartare (114). Instead of pâté de foie gras, slices of cold chicken, turkey, sweetbreads, or lobster may be used. The receipt for this jelly is given as it is generally made in this country, where gelatine is much used.

279. **Aspic** (another manner of making it). Cut in slices two onions and a carrot, put them in a saucepan on the fire, with two cloves, two pepper-corns, two bay-leaves, a branch of thyme, a few very thin slices of ham on top, four pounds of a knuckle of veal, two pounds of the lean part of a shin of beef, half a glass of water, and the remains of cold chicken or turkey. When beginning to color, moisten with three quarts of consommé (Art. 1), add two calf's feet, which you have boiled ten minutes in boiling water. Simmer very gently for four hours, remove all grease, and strain it through a flannel. Put it back again on the fire, mix the whites of four eggs with a glass of water, add it to your stock, also adding three wineglasses of sherry. Simmer gently at the back of the range for half an hour, strain it through a flannel until perfectly clear, and put it on the ice. This receipt is given in the manner in which aspic is made in France.

280. **Boned Chicken.** Boned chicken is prepared exactly in the same manner as boned turkey (Art. 292).

281. **Larded Chicken.** Prepare a chicken as for roasting, lard the breasts with pieces of larding pork, about an eighth of an inch wide and an inch and a half long. Put it in a saucepan with a sliced onion and carrot, six parsley-roots, two cloves, a clove of garlic, two pepper-corns, a branch of thyme, a bay-leaf, a pinch of salt, and enough consommé (stock, Art. 1) to cover three quarters of your chicken. When beginning to boil, send it to the oven for about an hour with all its liquid, with which baste it from time to time. Serve with a purée of artichokes (Art. 443), purée of celery (Art. 392 ), purée of French chestnuts (Art. 442), sauce Allemande (Art. 81), or other sauces preferred. You may also serve the chicken with a clear gravy. Grouse, partridges, and quail may be larded in the same manner.

282. **Chicken Pie à la Christine.** Clean two chickens, cut them in pieces, and put them in a saucepan with quarter of a pound of salt pork, an onion, and a little celery, all cut in small pieces, some salt, a pinch of pepper, a very little nutmeg, several branches of parsley, inclosing two bay-leaves, two branches of thyme, three cloves, and a clove of garlic, all tied together. Boil an hour, and skim off the grease carefully whenever necessary. Add two tablespoonfuls of flour with which you have thoroughly mixed half a glass of water, boil ten minutes longer, make a paste as for beefsteak pie (Art. 197), line a deep dish with it, in which put your chicken,

covering it on top with a round of paste the size of your dish, brush over it some beaten egg, and send to the oven, until well colored. Instead of celery, you may add some chopped mushrooms and truffles, and, instead of the pork, some small pieces of cooked ham, and hard-boiled eggs cut in slices.

283. **Chicken Croquettes.** Chop and pound fine in a mortar a pound of chicken from which you have removed all skin and sinews; also chop fine about ten mushrooms, which mix with your chicken, and add half a pint of Allemande sauce ([Art. 81](#)) rather thick, to which you have added the yolks of three eggs, mixed in two tablespoonfuls of water or milk. Put your mixture on the ice until perfectly cold, then form it into croquettes, which roll in bread-crumbs. Beat up three eggs, with which cover your croquettes; again roll in bread-crumbs. Put some lard in a frying-pan in which, when very hot, fry your croquettes, and, when a bright yellow color, drain, and serve with fried parsley on top. You may add to your mixture, before forming into croquettes, some chopped truffles or chopped parsley.

284. **Puff Paste.** Put a pound of flour on a table, make a hole in the center of the flour, in which by degrees pour half a pint of cold water. The water should always be added in very small quantities at a time, and thoroughly worked into the flour until perfectly absorbed before adding more. When all the water has been thoroughly mixed with the flour, work your paste out with the hands until round. Take a pound of butter, which has been on the ice, and which you have carefully washed. If very hard, knead it a little with your hands, then place it in the middle of your paste, flatten it, fold your paste over the butter so that it forms a square, and put it on the ice ten minutes. Then with a rolling-pin roll out your paste (having previously sprinkled the table with flour) about two feet long, then fold it one third of its length, roll it once with the rolling-pin, then take the remainder of the paste and fold it over the two other layers, and roll the paste two or three times, fold the paste again as before, and put it on the ice fifteen minutes. Then proceed as before, and put it again on the ice. Repeat the same operation once again.

285. **Pâté Brisée.** Put a pound of flour on a table, make a hollow in the middle of the flour, in which put eight ounces of butter and not quite half a pint of water. Work this paste well, so as to be quite smooth.

286. **Bouchées de Salpicon.** Take half a pound of puff paste, and, after having given it six turns, roll it out half an inch thick, cut it out in ten rounds, with a muffin-ring or a mold for the purpose. Mark lightly in the center of each, with the point of a knife, a very small round. Brush them (with a camel's-hair brush) in beaten egg, put them on a pan, send them to a very hot oven, and watch them carefully so that they do not color too much on the outside before the inside is done. This paste should rise at least two inches. When the bouchées are thoroughly done inside, and colored bright yellow on the outside, take them out of the oven, remove the small rounds in the center which you have marked out, and also enough paste from the inside to make space for the following mixture: Put half a pint of Spanish sauce (Art. 80), with a glass of sherry, in a saucepan on the fire, boil it ten minutes, then add eight mushrooms, four chickens' livers, which you have previously blanched in boiling water ten minutes, the breast of a cold chicken, some cold smoked tongue, and two truffles, all cut in small pieces. When hot, fill your bouchées, place the small covers on top of each, and serve. Instead of Spanish sauce, Allemande sauce (Art. 81) is often preferred. You may also add four ounces of chicken farce (Art. 11), which form into small balls, and poach in boiling water. Instead of chicken, you may substitute sweetbreads; or you may fill the bouchées with oysters, to which you have added an Allemande sauce and some mushrooms cut in small pieces.

287. **Croüstades de Salpicon.** Take some pâté brisée (Art. 285), roll it out very thin, butter ten little tin molds, which line with your paste, prick a few holes in the bottom and fill the insides, and send them to a hot oven until done, take them out of the molds, brush the outsides with beaten egg, put them back in the oven for five minutes, remove the flour from the insides, using a small, dry brush, so that none shall remain, and fill them with the mixture described in the foregoing article.

288. **Cromesqui of Chicken.** Make a mixture as for chicken croquettes (Art. 283), adding a little red pepper. When cold, form it into balls, about the size of a small egg, and wrap up each one in a very thin piece of pork. Break three eggs in a bowl, add six ounces of flour, mix well together, and then add a little water, so as to make a smooth and very soft paste, but sufficiently solid to adhere to your cromesqui. Then mix thoroughly a teaspoonful of soda with your paste, with which cover each cromesqui, and

fry in very hot lard. When a bright yellow, drain, and serve plain, or with a tomato sauce (Art. 90 ).

289. **Timbale of Chicken.** Chop fine, and then pound in a mortar half a pound of the white meat of chicken, from which you have removed the skin and sinews; add to the chicken, little by little, while pounding, three sherry-glasses of *very* cold cream, a little salt, white pepper, and the whites of five eggs. When you have obtained a very fine, smooth paste, press it through a sieve, and then fill with it ten little tin molds, which you have buttered. Place them in a saucepan, in which you have put the depth of an inch of water, cover your saucepan, and send to the oven for about ten minutes, or until the mixture is firm enough to turn out of the molds. Then serve with a sauce périgueux (Art. 91), or a sauce suprême (Art. 99), or a sauce Allemande (Art. 81 ).

290. **Roast Turkey stuffed.** Clean and prepare a medium-sized turkey for roasting. Cut two onions in pieces, and put them in a saucepan with two ounces of lard, and color them lightly. Soak a pound of bread in water, from which press the water, add the bread to your onions, with the turkey's liver and heart chopped very fine, a little salt, two pinches of pepper, the same of sage, a pinch of thyme, and mix all well together. Stuff the inside of the turkey with this mixture, sew up the opening through which you have introduced the stuffing, and put it to roast, with a little butter on top, and a wineglass of water. Roast for three quarters of an hour, strain the liquid in your pan, pour it over your turkey, and serve.

291. **Turkey with Truffles.** Clean and prepare a young medium-sized turkey as the foregoing. Melt four ounces of the fat of your turkey in a frying pan with a shallot and a few truffles chopped fine, a pinch of thyme, salt, pepper, and nutmeg, a pound of sausage-meat, and a can of truffles cut in quarters. Mix all well together, and with this mixture stuff your turkey; sew up the opening through which you have put your farce. Roast the turkey for three quarters of an hour, putting a little butter on the breast and a glass of white wine in the pan, and baste it often. Serve your turkey on a dish, and pour over it the liquid in your pan, which you have strained. Proceed in the same manner for chickens, capons, partridges, etc.—the quantity of each ingredient in proportion to the size of the piece roasted.

292. **Boned Turkey.** Take a hen-turkey of seven pounds, singe off the hair, by passing it over some lighted alcohol, cut off the head and neck, make an incision through the back its entire length, cut off the wings, and remove all the bones of the turkey. Take three pounds of chopped sausage-meat, the half of which place in the interior of your turkey, cover the farce with alternate strips of larding pork, half an inch wide, strips of cold ham, tongue, and some truffles cut in pieces intermixed. Season with pepper. Place on top of these the other half of your sausage-meat, which cover with another layer of larding pork, ham, and truffles. Then draw the meat at the sides to the center of the back of your turkey, and sew them together with a larding-needle threaded with fine twine. Place on top several slices of lemon, from which you have removed the peel and seeds, and wrap up your turkey very tight in a cloth, which tie firmly with a string, and put in a saucepan, in which you have put the bones of your turkey, a carrot, an onion, a little thyme, two bay-leaves, two cloves, one clove of garlic, and enough consommé (stock, [Art. 1](#)) to cover the turkey. Simmer gently for three hours, then remove the cloth, which wash clean, and again wrap the turkey in it, tying it as tight as possible. Place it in a pan, put another pan on top, in which put a weight, so as to render the top of the turkey perfectly flat, and put on ice for a day. Skim off the grease from the liquid in which your turkey was cooked, strain, take of it three pints, which put on the fire with three ounces of gelatine and the juice of two lemons. Mix four whites of eggs with a glass of water, pour into your saucepan with the stock and gelatine, stir all well together, and when beginning to boil remove to the back of the range to simmer gently for half an hour, strain through a flannel until perfectly clear, add a wineglass of sherry, put on the ice until cold, cut in pieces, which place on top and around your turkey.

293. **Tame Ducks roasted.** Clean and prepare two ducks for roasting. Put them in a pan with a little salt, a little butter, a wineglass of water, and roast them by a good fire for about twenty-five or thirty minutes. When well colored, serve them, surrounded with water-cresses. Strain the liquor in your pan, and serve in a sauce-boat with your ducks.

294. **Ducks with Olives.** Prepare and cook your ducks as the foregoing. Put half a pint of Spanish sauce ([Art. 80](#)) in a saucepan, let it boil, and add three dozen olives from which you have removed the stones, and a glass of

sherry; boil gently ten minutes, pour your sauce around your ducks, and serve.

295. **Duck with Turnips.** Prepare two ducks as the foregoing. Put in a saucepan a sliced onion and carrot, two pieces of larding pork, three bay-leaves, three branches of thyme, two cloves of garlic, four parsley-roots, three cloves, three pepper-corns, and a pinch of salt. Place your ducks on top, moisten them with sufficient consommé (Art. 1) to barely cover them, and a claret-glass of white wine. Boil very gently for an hour. Pare some turnips, cut them round and small, in sufficient quantity for eight people. Put them in a saucepan on the fire, with an ounce of lard; when equally colored, drain them, and place them in a saucepan with half a pint of Spanish sauce (Art. 80), a pinch of sugar, a pinch of pepper; boil until the turnips are done. Place your ducks on a dish, and your sauce, with the turnips, around them.

296. **Ducks with Purée of Peas.** Clean, prepare, and cook two ducks as the foregoing. Boil a quart of peas, put them through a sieve, then heat them in a saucepan with a little butter, salt, and a pinch of sugar, and serve, with your ducks, on a separate dish.

297. **Roast Goose.** Clean and prepare a young goose for roasting. Put a little butter on top, a little salt, and a claret-glass of water in your pan, and roast for an hour. Put half a pint of Spanish sauce in a saucepan on the fire, mix with it a tablespoonful of mustard, a teaspoonful of vinegar, a pinch of pepper, and nutmeg. Let it boil a moment, and serve, with your goose, in a sauce-boat.

298. **Braised Goose, Celery Sauce.** Prepare a goose as for duck with turnips (Art. 295). Cut a bunch of celery in small pieces, wash them well, and boil in water, with a little salt; when done, drain them. Put in a saucepan half a pint of white sauce (Art. 84), add your celery, boil five minutes, drain off your goose, pour your celery sauce on a dish, place your goose on top, and serve.

299. **Roast Squabs.** Clean and wash eight squabs, put a little butter and salt on top, and roast them thirty minutes. Reduce half a pint of consommé (Art. 1) on the fire, one half pour over your squabs, and serve some water-cresses around them.

300. **Broiled Squabs.** Clean and wash eight squabs, split them in two, flatten them with a cleaver, beat up two eggs, add an ounce of melted butter, a pinch of salt and pepper, mix all well together, spread over your squabs, and sprinkle them with bread-crumbs. Broil them on a gentle fire, and, when well colored, serve.

301. **Squabs en Compote.** Clean eight squabs, split them in two, put them in a saucepan with four ounces of butter, in small pieces. Color them slightly on the fire, and, when a good color, drain off the grease. Moisten your squabs with half a pint of Spanish sauce (Art. 80), add a pinch of pepper, nutmeg, and thyme, a glass of sherry, and boil thirty minutes. Peel two dozen little onions, toss them in a frying-pan with half an ounce of lard, and, when well colored, add them to your squabs. Cut a dozen mushrooms in quarters, boil ten minutes, and serve very hot.

302. **Broiled Squabs (Deviled).** Prepare exactly as for deviled chicken (Art. 266).

303. **Squabs with Green Peas.** Clean eight squabs, separate them in two, put them in a saucepan on the fire, with an ounce of butter. When a nice color, add half a glass of water, two bay-leaves, two branches of thyme, two cloves, two pepper-corns, a clove of garlic, and a pinch of salt and pepper. Cook thirty minutes, drain and strain the liquid in which your squabs were cooked, add to it a quart of boiled peas, and serve with your squabs.

304. **Broiled Partridge.** Clean and divide in two, for broiling, three partridges, break the thigh-bone, and broil them on a gentle fire. When well colored on both sides, serve them on a dish on which you have put two ounces of melted butter, a tablespoonful of chopped parsley, a pinch of pepper and salt, and the juice of a lemon, all well mixed together. Garnish with water-cresses or slices of lemon.

305. **Deviled Partridge.** Broil three partridges as the foregoing, and proceed as for deviled chicken (Art. 266).

306. **Partridge aux Choux.** Clean three partridges, and put them in a saucepan with half a pound of bacon, two smoked sausages, a carrot cut in two, and a whole onion, several branches of parsley, inclosing four cloves,

three branches of thyme, and a clove of garlic. Tie all well together, and cover your partridges with pieces of larding pork. Blanch a cabbage in boiling water on the fire for fifteen minutes, then put it for a moment in cold water, drain it, and press from it all moisture. Lay it on top of your partridges, and cover with strips of larding pork. Moisten with sufficient consommé (Art. 1 ) to cover them. Simmer gently for two hours. Drain off your partridges, bacon, sausages, and cabbage, from which again press the moisture. Remove your carrot, onion, and herbs, boil, and serve your partridges on a dish, with your cabbage underneath, and your bacon and sausage, cut in pieces, around them.

307. **Roast Partridge.** Clean three partridges, pass a wooden skewer through the thighs, tie on top of each a thin slice of pork, and roast them forty minutes. Put a claret-glass of white wine in the pan, and baste them from time to time. Remove your skewers, and the strings with which you have tied on your pork, and put your partridges on a dish. Add two wineglasses of consommé (Art. 1) to the liquid in the pan, boil for a moment, strain and pour in the dish with your partridges, which serve, garnished with water-cresses, or with bread sauce (Art. 87 ).

308. **Salmi of Partridge.** Cut up in pieces three cold roast partridges, which put in a saucepan with an onion cut in slices, two cloves, a bay-leaf, a branch of thyme, a clove of garlic, two parsley-roots, and six chopped mushrooms. Moisten with a claret-glass of white wine, and half a pint of Spanish sauce (Art. 80). Boil very gently for half an hour, carefully removing all grease, and strain. Then put your sauce again in the saucepan with your partridges, add two dozen mushrooms, and keep them hot. Fry a bright yellow, in butter, eight pieces of bread, cut round at one end and pointed at the other; drain them. Serve your partridges, the sauce poured over them, and garnish with your fried pieces of bread.

309. **Truffled Partridge.** Prepare three partridges as for roasting, make an incision in the skin of the neck. Pound together two chickens' livers and the same in quantity of fresh fat pork, adding a pinch of salt and pepper and a little nutmeg. Mix all together, with half a pound of truffles, cut in quarters, and put the third of your farce in each partridge. Sew up the opening through which you have inserted the farce, and also the skin of the neck. Then put a little butter on them, and roast them for thirty-five to forty

minutes, according to the size of your partridges. Serve around them a sauce périgueux (Art. 91 ). Grouse are prepared in each manner described for partridges.

310. **Broiled Quail.** Prepare and broil eight quails as for broiled partridge. You may also devil them, as described in deviled chicken (Art. 266).

311. **Roast Quail.** Prepare eight quails for roasting, with a piece of thin pork on top and a claret-glass of consommé (Art. 1) in the pan. Fifteen minutes on a good fire will be sufficient to roast them. Boil the liquid in your pan for a moment, strain it, put it in a dish with your quails, under each of which you have placed a piece of toast, and serve garnished with watercresses.

312. **Quail en Caisse.** Split eight quails through the back, without injuring the fillets, and remove the bones. Take half a dozen chickens' livers with as much fat pork, and pound together to a paste, then mix with this four truffles chopped very fine, salt, pepper, and nutmeg, and fill the inside of your quail with this mixture, then wrap them up in thin strips of pork, and tie a string around each, so as to preserve their shape. Put them in a pan and send them to the oven for fifteen minutes. Then take eight paper cases, as wide and as high as your quail, put a little oil on the inside of the cases, and half fill them with a farce of sausage, with which you have mixed four chopped truffles, as many mushrooms, a little salt, pepper, and nutmeg. Put your quail on top, and send them to the oven for twenty minutes. Put a tablespoonful of Spanish sauce (Art. 80) on top of each quail.

313. **Quail with Truffles.** Clean eight quails, split them through the back and remove the bones. Put in a saucepan on the fire for a moment the livers of your quails, five chickens' livers, and the same quantity of fresh fat pork. Take them out of your saucepan and pound them together, adding two truffles chopped fine, a pinch of salt, pepper, and nutmeg, fill your quails with the mixture and sew up the opening. Tie on top of each a thin piece of pork, place them in a saucepan with slices of ham, and moisten half their height with an equal quantity of consommé (Art. 1) and white wine. Send them to the oven for about thirty minutes, remove the strings used for tying on the pork, and place your quails on a dish. Skim off all grease from their

liquid, strain it, put it in a saucepan on the fire for a moment, add to it a dozen truffles cut in slices, pour it over your quails, and serve.

314. **Pigeons Poêlés.** Clean eight pigeons, and put them in a saucepan with a clove of garlic, two cloves, two pepper-corns, two bay-leaves, a branch of thyme, an onion cut in slices, a little salt and pepper, and moisten with quarter of a pint of consommé and the same of white wine. Simmer gently, and, when they are cooked, drain off the liquid, remove all the grease, strain it, reduce it on the fire one half, add a dozen mushrooms, and serve with the pigeons.

315. **Pigeons en Compote.** Prepare and cook eight pigeons in the same manner as described for squabs en compote (Art. 301), with the exception of cooking them an hour longer.

316. **Fillets of Hare Sautés.** Take the fillets of two hares, and cut them in medium-sized pieces. Put them in a saucepan with two ounces of butter, an onion cut in slices, a clove of garlic chopped, two bay-leaves, two cloves, and two branches of thyme. After having been on a good fire ten minutes, add a tablespoonful of flour and your fillets; moisten with quarter of a pint of consommé (Art. 1), and the same of red wine, a pinch of salt and pepper, and boil on a good fire forty minutes. Remove your fillets, strain the liquid, put it back on the fire with your fillets, add a tablespoonful of vinegar, boil five minutes, and serve.

317. **Roast Hare.** Clean and uncase a hare, then take off the skin on top of the thighs and fillet, lard them, and put them in a pan with a little salt and pepper on top and a little melted butter. Baste them from time to time, and roast them an hour. Serve with a sauce poivrade (Art. 95).

318. **Hare à la Bourgeoise.** When your hare is uncased and cleaned, cut it in pieces and put it in a saucepan, with a quarter of a pound of bacon cut in small pieces, several branches of parsley, inclosing three cloves, three pepper-corns, two branches of thyme, two cloves of garlic, and tie all well together. Moisten with half a pint of consommé (Art. 1 ), the same of white wine, and about thirty pieces of turnips cut in small quarters; reduce on the fire until nearly all the liquid has evaporated, and serve.

319. **Ragoût of Hare.** Skin and clean a hare, cut it in pieces and prepare it in the same manner as for ragoût of venison (Art. 331).

320. **Rabbit Sauté à la Minute.** Cut in pieces two rabbits, which you have skinned and cleaned, put them in a saucepan with two ounces of butter, salt, pepper, a little allspice, and nutmeg. Put on the fire for about twenty minutes, then add four chopped shallots, a wineglass of white wine, boil ten minutes, add a tablespoonful of chopped parsley, and serve.

321. **Ragoût of Rabbit.** After having cleaned and skinned two rabbits, cut them in pieces and cook exactly as for ragoût of venison (Art. 331).

322. **Roast Rabbit.** Take two rabbits and proceed exactly as for roast hare, except that instead of cooking an hour, cook them three quarters of an hour, and serve with a sauce ravigote hot (Art. 111).

323. **Hash of Rabbit.** Take the remains of two rabbits, or one whole rabbit, and the same quantity of a cold leg of mutton, and chop very fine. Break the bones of your rabbit and put them in a saucepan, with two chopped cloves of garlic, two cloves, two bay-leaves, a branch of thyme, a little mace, and a pinch of sage. Put them on the fire ten minutes, moisten with two claret-glasses of red wine and one of consommé (Art. 1). Boil three quarters of an hour, strain, then add them to your hash in a frying-pan, with a little salt, pepper, and nutmeg. Heat without boiling, and serve very hot; garnish with pieces of bread fried in butter.

324. **Rabbit à l'Espagnole.** After having skinned and cleaned two rabbits, cut them in pieces and put them in a saucepan on the fire for fifteen minutes with some butter. Moisten them with a claret-glass of consommé (Art. 1), a pinch of salt, pepper, and nutmeg, and a little thyme. Reduce on the fire until almost all moisture is evaporated, add half a pint of Spanish sauce (Art. 80), and three tablespoonfuls of tomatoes. Boil ten minutes, and just before serving sprinkle a little chopped parsley on top.

325. **Suprême of Partridge.** Take the breasts of four partridges and separate the upper from the lower fillet, so as to make an opening for stuffing; chop up the white and dark meat fine, which put in a saucepan with a little butter, and toss on the fire until done; then mix thoroughly with quarter of a pint of béchamel sauce (Art. 83), and a few truffles and

mushrooms chopped fine. When this mixture is cold, stuff with it the under fillet of partridge and cover with the upper. Put them in a pan, cover with buttered paper, and send to a moderate oven for about half an hour, or a little more. Dust over with hashed truffles, and serve with purée of celery (Art. 392).

326. **Timbale of Partridge.** Proceed exactly as for timbale of chicken (Art. 289). Timbale of grouse may be made in the same manner.

327. **Venison Chops, with Currant Jelly Sauce.** Broil eight venison chops for about six to seven minutes. Put in a saucepan nearly half a pint of Spanish sauce (Art. 80) and the eighth of a pint of currant jelly; let them boil a moment, or until the currant jelly is dissolved; then serve your chops with the sauce around them.

328. **Saddle of Venison.** Take seven pounds of a saddle of venison, roast it about thirty-five minutes, and serve with currant jelly.

329. **Leg of Venison.** Take seven pounds of a leg of venison, which roast forty-five minutes, and serve with currant jelly.

330. **Venison Chops.** Put eight venison chops in an earthen jar with four bay-leaves, three branches of thyme, six cloves, six pepper-corns, four branches of parsley, a clove of garlic, a sliced onion and carrot, and a pint of vinegar; let them soak twenty-four hours; drain them, and put them in a frying-pan with an ounce of butter; shake them in the pan until done. Put four tablespoonfuls of vinegar, with a pinch of pepper, in a saucepan on the fire, reduce two thirds, add half a pint of Spanish sauce (Art. 80), boil five minutes, and serve with your chops on a very hot dish.

331. **Ragoût of Venison.** Cut into pieces three pounds of a breast of venison, which put on the fire in a saucepan, with half a pound of bacon cut in small pieces, and a little salt, pepper, and nutmeg, for fifteen minutes; mix well with your ingredients two tablespoonfuls of flour, add half a pint of consommé (stock), and the same of red wine; also several branches of parsley, inclosing three cloves, three pepper-corns, two branches of thyme, two bay-leaves, a clove of garlic, and tie all together. Boil three quarters of an hour. Peel two dozen white onions, color them in a frying-pan on the

fire, with a little butter, and then add them to your stew; boil fifteen minutes longer, add a dozen mushrooms cut in quarters, and serve.

332. **Braised Fillets of Venison.** Put four fillets of venison in an earthen jar, with half a pint of oil, a little salt, pepper, and nutmeg, for four hours; drain them and put them in a saucepan on the fire, with two cloves, two pepper-corns, two bay-leaves, two branches of thyme, a pinch of salt and pepper, and a sliced onion. Moisten with an equal quantity of consommé (stock, Art. 1) and white wine, so as to almost cover your fillets. Simmer gently for an hour and a half; drain them, and serve with a sauce piquante (Art. 86).

333. **Broiled Plover.** Clean eight plovers, split them down the back without separating the two parts; chop the livers very fine, add half of their quantity of butter, as much bread-crumbs which you have pressed through a sieve, a little salt, pepper, nutmeg, a pinch of thyme, either powdered or chopped very fine, the white of an egg, and a tablespoonful of parsley chopped very fine. Mix all thoroughly together, toast eight pieces of bread without the crust, spread your mixture upon them; broil the plovers, place them on top of your toast, and serve garnished with water-cresses.

334. **Roast Plover.** Prepare and clean eight plovers for roasting; tie on top of each a thin piece of pork; and roast them twenty minutes. Remove the strings and place the plovers on a dish; take the liquid from the pan in which the birds were roasted, add a wineglass of consommé (Art. 1 ), boil for a moment, strain, and pour it on the dish with the plovers; serve garnished with water-cresses.

335. **Broiled Woodcock.** Prepare eight woodcocks for broiling; preserve the insides, except the gizzard, chop them, finish as for the toast described in broiled plover (Art. 333), and serve garnished with slices of lemon.

336. **Roast Woodcock.** Prepare as for roast plover. Roast them twelve to fifteen minutes.

337. **Snipe.** Snipe are prepared as woodcocks, robins, and other small birds.

338. **Reed-Birds.** Take two dozen reed-birds and put them in a saucepan, with two ounces of butter, a pinch of salt and pepper, toss them in the pan, on a quick fire, for about three minutes. Put them on a dish on which you have placed pieces of toast; add a wineglass of consommé (Art. 1) to the butter in your saucepan. Boil a moment, strain, add the juice of a lemon, and pour over the reed-birds. Reed-birds are also roasted, served on toast, with sometimes a silver skewer passed through them. Four to five minutes, on a good fire, will be sufficient to roast them.

339. **Roast Canvas-Back Ducks.** Prepare and clean four canvas-back ducks, pass them over some lighted alcohol to singe the hair; wash them well, and do not cut off the heads. Pass a skewer through the thighs and under the wings, and put them before the fire for fifteen minutes to roast. Take out the skewers, garnish with water-cresses, and serve some currant jelly separately.

340. **Red-Head Ducks.** Prepare and cook as the foregoing.

341. **Broiled Red-Head Ducks.** After having cleaned and washed three red-head ducks, split them in two for broiling, and, when well-colored on both sides, serve them with a sauce poivrade (Art. 95), sauce piquante (Art. 86), or other sharp, highly-seasoned sauces.

342. **Salmi of Red-Head Ducks.** Take the remains of three red-head ducks, or two whole red-head, cold, cut up in pieces, and finish as for salmi of partridge (Art. 308). Mallard, teal, and other wild ducks are prepared as described in the foregoing articles on ducks; the time necessary to roast them depending on their size.

# CHAPTER V.
## *VEGETABLES.*

343. **Green Peas à l'Anglaise.** Put a quart of water in a saucepan with a pinch of salt; when boiling, add three pints of green peas, and boil them for twenty-five minutes; take one out and see if thoroughly done, if so, drain them, and put them in a saucepan with two ounces of butter, a pinch of salt and sugar, and serve them very hot.

344. **Green Peas à la Française.** Put three pints of green peas in a saucepan, with ten branches of parsley tied together, a whole onion peeled, a pinch of salt and sugar, and a pint of water. Boil for twenty-five minutes, and, if sufficiently done, take out the onion and parsley. Mix on a table an ounce of butter with a teaspoonful of flour, which add to your peas on the fire, stir gently with a spoon, and, when thoroughly mixed and the butter dissolved, serve very hot.

345. **Green Peas with Bacon.** Cut the rind from a quarter of a pound of bacon, which cut in small pieces and place in a saucepan on the fire, when beginning to color add a tablespoonful of flour, a little pepper and nutmeg, and ten branches of parsley tied together; moisten with a glass of water; add three pints of green peas, and boil about thirty minutes; if sufficiently done, remove the bunch of parsley, and serve. Peas cooked in this way are often used as a garnish for different kinds of meat.

346. **Green Peas à la Paysanne.** Put three pints of green peas in a saucepan, with an ounce of butter, ten branches of parsley tied together, a whole onion peeled, a pinch of sugar, a little salt, half a glass of water, a lettuce cut in pieces (as for Julienne soup). Simmer very gently, and, when the peas are sufficiently done, mix three yolks of eggs with three tablespoonfuls of cream, and, having removed your parsley and onion, add the eggs to your peas; mix all well together, and serve.

347. **String-Beans à l'Anglaise.** Take three pints of string-beans, string them, and put them in nearly two quarts of boiling water, in which you have

put a little salt; when the beans are sufficiently cooked, drain them and put them in a saucepan with two ounces of butter, a pinch of salt, a very little chopped parsley, the juice of a lemon, and serve them very hot.

348. **String-Beans Sautés.** Prepare and cook your beans as the foregoing. Put in a saucepan three ounces of butter, a pinch of salt, the juice of a lemon, a tablespoonful of chopped parsley, and six tablespoonfuls of sauce Allemande ([Art. 81](#)); mix all well together, pour over your beans, and serve hot.

349. **Beans Panachés.** Prepare a pint and a half of string-beans, as the preceding; put in a saucepan two quarts of water, a good pinch of salt, and boil them until tender. Take the same of white beans, which boil; drain them both and put them in a saucepan together, adding a pinch of salt, three ounces of butter, the juice of a lemon, and a tablespoonful of chopped parsley; when very hot, serve.

350. **White Beans Sautés.** Boil three pints of beans as the foregoing, and, when they are thoroughly done, drain them and put them in a saucepan with three ounces of butter, a pinch of salt and pepper, a tablespoonful of chopped parsley, and the juice of half a lemon; serve very hot. You may also add, after removing your saucepan from the fire, the yolks of two eggs well mixed in two tablespoonfuls of milk or cream.

351. **Dried Beans.** Soak, the night before they are required to use, three pints of dried beans, and proceed as for the preceding. The time required to cook them depends on the quality of your beans.

352. **Purée of Dried Beans.** Soak in water for twelve hours a quart of dried beans, drain them, and put them in a saucepan with boiling water and a little salt. When thoroughly cooked, press them through a sieve, and then put them in a saucepan with three ounces of butter; when very hot, serve.

353. **Red Beans.** Soak in water for twelve hours three pints of red beans; then boil them in two quarts of water, with an onion, a carrot, a pinch of sugar and pepper, several branches of parsley, inclosing two cloves, two branches of thyme, tied all together, half a pound of bacon, and half a pint of red wine; when your beans have absorbed all moisture, remove your

carrot, onion, and branch of parsley, add two ounces of butter, and serve, with the bacon cut in slices, around your beans.

354. **Windsor Beans.** Put three pints of very small Windsor beans in two quarts of boiling water, a good pinch of salt, and a branch of savory herb. When your beans are thoroughly cooked, drain them and put them in a saucepan, with a pinch of salt, pepper, sugar, nutmeg, and a tablespoonful of savory herb chopped very fine. Mix two eggs in two tablespoonfuls of milk or cream, and add them to your beans, after having taken them off the fire. If, instead of small beans, you have large ones, the skin or peel must be removed.

355. **Windsor Beans à l'Anglaise.** Prepare and cook your beans as the foregoing, and, just before serving, add a tablespoonful of mint chopped very fine.

356. **Purée of Windsor Beans.** Boil three quarts of Windsor beans in consommé ([Art. 1](#)), with a bunch of savory herb, and a little salt; when thoroughly done, press them through a sieve, and then put them in a saucepan on the fire with three ounces of butter, a pinch of sugar, and two wineglasses of good cream. Serve very hot, garnished with pieces of bread fried in butter.

357. **Asparagus with French Rolls.** Cut off the tops of eight oval, soft, French rolls, remove the inside, in which put a little butter, and send to the oven for three or four minutes to color lightly. Fill them with the green ends of about three bunches of asparagus, which you have previously boiled, and about half a pint of sauce Allemande ([Art. 81](#)), well mixed with the asparagus ends. Serve very hot.

358. **Asparagus with Butter Sauce.** Scrape and wash two bunches of asparagus, cut them in equal lengths, and put them in two quarts of boiling water, with a little salt. Boil them until perfectly tender, drain and serve them very hot, with a white sauce ([Art. 84](#)), or with melted butter.

359. **Pointes d'Asperges au Veloutée.** Cut the green ends, about an inch in length, of three bunches of asparagus, and put them in three pints of boiling water, with two pinches of salt. Boil rapidly for about ten minutes, and, when thoroughly done, drain them, and put them in a saucepan with

two ounces of butter, a pinch of salt, pepper, nutmeg, two pinches of sugar, and about six tablespoonfuls of sauce veloutée (Art. 82). Mix all well together, and serve very hot.

360. **Asperges en Petits Pois.** Cut off in pieces about the size of a pea the green ends of four bunches of asparagus, which put in two quarts of boiling water, and half an ounce of salt. Boil them rapidly, and, when thoroughly cooked, drain them, and put them in a saucepan with two ounces of butter, a little nutmeg, two pinches of sugar, and six tablespoonfuls of béchamel sauce (Art. 83). Mix all well together, and serve garnished with pieces of bread fried in butter.

361. **Lentils.** Clean and wash two quarts of lentils, and boil them in two quarts of boiling water, and a little salt. When thoroughly cooked, drain them, and finish as for white beans (Art. 350).

362. **Cauliflower with Butter Sauce.** Take some cauliflowers, in quantity according to size, wash them, trim off the leaves, and put them in two quarts of boiling water on the fire, adding half an ounce of salt, half an ounce of butter, and the juice of a lemon. Boil rapidly until quite tender, drain, and serve them with a white sauce (Art. 84).

363. **Cauliflower au Gratin.** Boil your cauliflowers as the foregoing, then put them in a deep dish, add half a pint of sauce Allemande (Art. 81), in which you have mixed four ounces of grated cheese. Sprinkle thickly with bread-crumbs, and a little melted butter, and send to the oven until colored a light brown.

364. **Cauliflower au Veloutée.** Prepare as for cauliflowers with butter sauce (Art. 362), and serve with a sauce veloutée (Art. 82).

365. **Artichokes with Butter Sauce.** Take eight artichokes, cut off the stalks, and also about half an inch off the leaves; then place them in three quarts of boiling water and half an ounce of salt, and boil about half an hour; pass the point of a knife through the bottom of one, and, if soft, the artichoke is sufficiently done. Drain, and serve with a white or butter sauce (Art. 84).

366. **Fonds d'Artichauts à l'Italienne.** Cut off the stalks, remove the leaves and the furze in the inside of eight artichokes, boil them as the

foregoing, and serve with an Italian sauce (Art. 93).

367. **Fonds d'Artichauts à la Macédoine.** Cut off the stalks, remove all the leaves from eight artichokes, and also the furze which adheres to the bottom. Trim them perfectly round, and put them in three pints of boiling water, with a little salt, and, when thoroughly done, drain them, fill them with a macédoine of vegetables (Art. 416), and serve them very hot.

368. **Fried Artichokes.** Take eight artichokes, cut off the stalks and the ends of the leaves, and put them in a bowl for an hour, with half a glass of vinegar, and a little salt and pepper. Break three eggs in a bowl, to which add two ounces of flour, a pinch of pepper and salt; drain off your artichokes, dip them in your eggs and flour, and fry them one by one in hot lard; drain them, and serve very hot.

369. **Artichokes à la Barrigoule.** Prepare and boil eight artichokes; when done, drain them and remove the leaves in the middle, also the furze which adheres to the bottom of the artichokes; let them dry thoroughly; cover a frying-pan about half an inch deep with oil; when very hot, add your artichokes, the tips of the leaves touching the oil; when a fine color, drain them. Chop fine four ounces of fat fresh pork, two shallots, a tablespoonful of parsley, and a dozen mushrooms; add a pinch of salt, pepper, and nutmeg, and a wineglass of sherry; mix all well together, and with this mixture fill the center of your artichokes. Tie a strip of thin pork on each and put them in a saucepan, on top of an onion and a carrot sliced extremely fine; moisten with a glass of consommé (Art. 1) and a claret-glass of white wine, heat them for a moment on the fire, send them to the oven for three quarters of an hour, remove the strips of pork, and fill the artichokes up to the top with Italian sauce (Art. 93).

370. **Raw Artichokes à la Vinaigrette.** Cut eight artichokes in thin slices; mix well together eight tablespoonfuls of oil, three tablespoonfuls of vinegar, a pinch of salt and pepper, and serve with your artichokes. Artichokes to be eaten raw must be very fresh.

371. **Jerusalem Artichokes.** Peel two dozen Jerusalem artichokes, boil them in two or three quarts of boiling water, with a pinch of salt; when thoroughly done, pour over them a sauce béchamel (Art. 83).

372. **Spinach à l'Anglaise.** Pick three quarts of spinach, wash it very carefully, changing the water several times; then put it in four quarts of boiling water, adding half an ounce of salt. Boil your spinach on a very hot fire, taking care to press it down into the saucepan from time to time; boil it for about ten minutes, then put it in cold water for a moment, and press the water from it; chop it rather fine and put it in a saucepan with six ounces of butter, a pinch of salt, a nutmeg, and serve very hot.

373. **Spinach à l'Espagnole.** Boil your spinach as the foregoing, and, after chopping it extremely fine, put it in a saucepan with four ounces of butter, a little salt and nutmeg, and an eighth of a pint of Spanish sauce ([Art. 80](#)); serve it very hot, garnished with pieces of bread fried in butter.

374. **Spinach with Cream.** Boil your spinach as the foregoing, chop it extremely fine. Put in a saucepan on the fire four ounces of butter, a tablespoonful of flour, a little salt, nutmeg, half a teaspoonful of sugar, and half a pint of cream. Stir all well together until boiling, add your spinach, and, when hot, serve, garnished with pieces of bread fried in butter.

375. **Salsify with Butter Sauce.** Scrape three bunches of salsify, dip them in three quarts of water and two tablespoonfuls of vinegar, to prevent their turning black, then cut them three inches in length. Put two tablespoonfuls of flour in a saucepan, add, by degrees, some water, stirring constantly, until two quarts have been added, then a tablespoonful of vinegar, a little salt, and your salsify. Boil about an hour, or until it is perfectly tender; drain, and serve with a white or butter sauce ([Art. 84](#)). Instead of butter sauce, you may serve with them a Spanish sauce ([Art. 80](#)), veloutée ([Art. 82](#)), or béchamel sauce ([Art. 83](#)).

376. **Fried Salsify.** Prepare and boil your salsify as above, cut them two inches in length, and when very tender drain them. Put in a bowl half a pound of flour, two eggs, and some water. Mix well together until you have a soft, smooth paste, thin enough to pour from a spoon. Cover each piece of salsify with the paste, and fry one by one in very hot lard, drain them, and serve them on a dish, piled one on top of the other.

377. **Stewed Tomatoes.** Put a can of tomatoes in a saucepan, with four ounces of butter, a little salt and pepper, a pinch of sugar, and two tablespoonfuls of bread-crumbs. Boil five minutes, and serve.

378. **Broiled Tomatoes.** Slice eight tomatoes, sprinkle them thickly with bread-crumbs and a little butter, broil them on a moderate fire, and, when a bright yellow color on top, serve them on a dish in a circle, one on top of the other.

379. **Farcied Tomatoes.** Take eight medium-sized, firm tomatoes, cut a hole on top of each, and scoop out the inside of the tomato, chop an onion, put it in a saucepan on the fire, with an ounce of butter, to simmer gently. When slightly colored, add six ounces of bread-crumbs, which you have soaked in water, and then pressed out nearly all the moisture, a dozen chopped mushrooms, a tablespoonful of chopped parsley, a pinch of salt, pepper, and thyme chopped fine, a little red pepper, and four tablespoonfuls of tomato sauce (Art. 90); mix all well together, and then fill the inside of your tomatoes. Sprinkle the tops of each with bread-crumbs and a little melted butter. Send them to the oven, and, when colored a light brown on top, serve, with a tomato sauce around them.

380. **Boiled Onions.** Peel a dozen medium-sized white onions, boil them in a quart of water with a little salt. When very tender, drain them, and serve with a butter sauce (Art. 84), or a sauce béchamel (Art. 83).

381. **Fried Onions.** Peel eight medium-sized onions, cut them in slices across the top, roll them in flour, fry them in hot lard, drain, and serve.

382. **Onions Glacés.** Peel a dozen small onions, color them lightly in a frying-pan on the fire with a little lard. Then put them in a saucepan with half a pint of consommé (stock, Art. 1), a pinch of salt, pepper, and nutmeg. Simmer very gently until the consommé is reduced three quarters, then pour it on a dish, your onions placed on top, and serve.

383. **Fried Egg-Plant.** Peel an egg-plant, cut it in slices about a third of an inch thick, dip them in three beaten eggs, to which you have added a pinch of salt and pepper. Sprinkle them with bread-crumbs, and fry them in very hot lard, drain, and serve them.

384. **Egg-Plant farcied.** Take four small egg-plants, peel them and separate them in two, scoop out the inside, which fill with a chicken farce (Art. 11), and sprinkle a few bread-crumbs on top. Cut an onion and a carrot in slices, and put them in a saucepan, with a branch of thyme, a bay-leaf,

two cloves, and a clove of garlic. Place your egg-plants on top. Moisten within three quarters of their height with consommé (stock, Art. 1), and a claret-glass of white wine. Put them in the oven for an hour, pouring over them, from time to time, some of the liquid in the pan. Pour over them half a pint of Spanish sauce (Art. 80), to which you have added a wineglass of sherry, and serve.

385. **Cucumbers farcied.** Divide four medium-sized cucumbers in two, after having pared them. Scoop out the inside and fill with a chicken farce (Art. 11). Put a sliced onion in a saucepan on the fire, with three slices of ham cut thin, place your cucumbers on top, moisten with a claret-glass of white wine, and the same of Spanish sauce (Art. 80 ). Then send them to the oven, pouring over them, from time to time, the liquid in the pan, which, when the cucumbers are sufficiently done, strain, pour over your cucumbers on a dish, and serve.

386. **Cucumbers with Cream.** Peel half a dozen cucumbers, cut them in medium-sized square pieces, soak them for two hours in some vinegar, and a pinch of salt. Turn them over from time to time, drain them, and dry them on a cloth, pressing the moisture from them. Put them in a saucepan on the fire, with an ounce of butter, half a pint of consommé (stock, Art. 1), several branches of parsley, inclosing two cloves, two branches of thyme, a clove of garlic, and tie all together, add a pinch of salt. When they are cooked, drain them, add them to half a pint of béchamel sauce (Art. 83), the juice of half a lemon, a tablespoonful of chopped parsley, and serve very hot.

387. **Lentils à la Maître d'Hôtel.** Wash three pints of lentils, put them in a saucepan with two quarts of water and a pinch of salt. Boil them very slowly for an hour, or until perfectly tender, then drain them, put them in a saucepan on the fire for a moment, with four ounces of butter, a little salt, a pinch of pepper, nutmeg, and a tablespoonful of chopped parsley. Remove your saucepan from the fire, mix the yolks of two eggs in two tablespoonfuls of water, add them to your lentils, mixing all well together, and serve.

388. **Purée of Lentils.** Prepare and boil as the foregoing, press them through a sieve, add about three ounces of butter, salt, pepper, and a very little nutmeg. Heat them on the fire for a few moments, and serve.

389. **Celery with Marrow.** Remove the green leaves from a bunch of celery, scrape the roots, cut the celery in pieces of about five inches long, wash them well, and put them in a saucepan, with plenty of water, and a little salt, and boil them ten minutes. Then put them in cold water for a moment. Cover the bottom of a saucepan with thin pieces of pork, a sliced onion and carrot, and several branches of parsley, inclosing three cloves, three pepper-corns, two bay-leaves, two branches of thyme, a clove of garlic, and tie all together, and then put your celery on top, nearly cover with consommé (stock, Art. 1), add the juice of a lemon, and place a buttered paper on top. Simmer gently for an hour and a half. Heat half a pint of Spanish sauce (Art. 80), with a glass of sherry, pour over your celery, and place on top some beef marrow, which you have previously soaked in water for four hours, then boiled ten minutes, and cut in round pieces the size of a fifty-cent piece.

390. **Celery with White Sauce.** Clean and wash a bunch of celery, which boil until tender, in plenty of water and a little salt, drain, and serve with a white or butter sauce (Art. 84), or a sauce Allemande (Art. 81).

391. **Fried Celery, Tomato Sauce.** Prepare and boil a bunch of celery as the foregoing; then drain it. Put in a bowl half a pound of flour, two eggs, and a little water. Mix well together until you have a soft, smooth paste, thin enough to pour from a spoon. Cut your celery into pieces about five inches long, cover them with your paste, fry them in hot lard until a light brown; drain, and serve with a tomato sauce (Art. 90).

392. **Purée of Celery.** Wash and clean two bunches of celery, cut them in pieces, and boil them in three quarts of water, with a little salt; when boiled thoroughly tender, drain, and add them to half a pint of béchamel sauce (Art. 83), a pinch of salt, pepper, and nutmeg. Boil ten minutes, press through a sieve, put back in the saucepan to heat again, and serve.

393. **Horse-Radish Sauce (cold).** Grate four ounces of horse-radish, to which add four ounces of bread-crumbs, and press through a sieve; add a glass of cream, a pinch of salt, and a tablespoonful of vinegar; mix all well together, and serve.

394. **Horse-Radish Sauce (hot).** Prepare the same as the above, adding two ounces of bread-crumbs, instead of four; heat all together in a

saucepan, and serve.

395. **Braised Lettuce, Madeira Sauce.** Wash eight lettuce, blanch them ten minutes in boiling water, then put them for a moment in cold water, and press out all the moisture. Spread thin pieces of pork on the bottom of a saucepan, a sliced carrot and onion, several branches of parsley, a little pepper, salt, and nutmeg, and the lettuce on top. Moisten three quarters of their height with consommé (stock, Art. 1), cover with a buttered paper, simmer gently two hours, drain them well, and serve them with half a pint of very hot Spanish sauce (Art. 80), to which you have added a wineglass of sherry or madeira.

396. **Farcied Lettuce.** Boil eight lettuce as the foregoing, and, after you have put them in cold water for a moment, dry them with a cloth and press out all the moisture; divide them partly in two, without allowing them to fall apart; place in each lettuce about two ounces of chicken farce (Art. 11), which cover with the leaves of your lettuce; shape them neatly, wrap them and tie them up in thin pieces of pork, and finish cooking as the foregoing; remove the pieces of pork, and serve with a Spanish sauce (Art. 80).

397. **Turnips with Cream.** Peel and boil in plenty of water and a little salt, ten white turnips; when very tender, drain them and pour over them half a pint of béchamel sauce (Art. 83), to which you have added two tablespoonfuls of cream.

398. **Purée of Turnips.** Peel and wash about fifteen white turnips, boil them in plenty of water and a little salt until perfectly tender; drain them, put them through a sieve, add two ounces of butter, a little salt, pepper, and nutmeg; and serve very hot.

399. **Turnips Glacés au Jus.** Peel and wash about ten white turnips, cut them perfectly round, boil them ten minutes, put them in cold water for a moment, then place them in a saucepan with a pinch of pepper, nutmeg, and sugar, and half a pint of consommé (stock, Art. 1). Simmer gently until perfectly tender; mix with the blade of a knife, on a table, half an ounce of butter and a teaspoonful of flour, which add to your turnips; boil for a few minutes, so as to mix thoroughly with your sauce, and serve.

400. **Beets with Butter.** Peel and wash a dozen small beets, boil them in three quarts of water, and, when perfectly tender, put them in cold water for a moment, cut them in thin slices, put them in a saucepan with two ounces of butter and a pinch of salt; serve very hot. You may also boil them and serve them with a sauce béchamel (Art. 83), to which you have added two tablespoonfuls of cream.

401. **Pickled Beets.** Boil ten medium-sized beets, cut them in slices, and put them in a bowl with six cloves, six pepper-corns, six bay-leaves, three cloves of garlic peeled, and half an ounce of salt; almost cover them with vinegar and water in equal quantity; serve very cold.

402. **Broiled Mushrooms.** Take some mushrooms, in quantity according to their size, peel them, wash, and then dry them on a cloth. Broil them on a gentle fire, a little butter on top, and, when colored on both sides, put an ounce of melted butter on a dish, the juice of lemon, a tablespoonful of chopped parsley, mix all well together, and serve your mushrooms on top; or serve the mushrooms singly on very hot toast, on which you have put a little butter.

403. **Stewed Mushrooms, Spanish Sauce.** Put half a pint of Spanish sauce (Art. 80) in a saucepan, with a sherry-glass of sherry, add your mushrooms, stew about five minutes, and serve.

404. **Stewed Mushrooms à la Princesse.** Put into a saucepan a gill of sauce Allemande (Art. 81 ), a glass of cream, a pinch of pepper, nutmeg, an ounce of butter, and the juice of a lemon, add some mushrooms, which you have peeled and washed, and a tablespoonful of chopped parsley. Boil for a few moments, and serve very hot.

405. **Mushrooms au Gratin.** Reduce on the fire ten minutes a cup of Allemande sauce (Art. 81), pour it over some mushrooms, in a deep dish, sprinkle with bread-crumbs, and pour a little melted butter on top, send to the oven, and, when colored a light brown, serve.

406. **Mushrooms au Gratin** (another way). Wash and cut off the stalks of about a dozen as large mushrooms as possible. Peel and chop fine an onion, which put in a saucepan on the fire, with an ounce of butter. Simmer very gently, and, when the onion is colored slightly, add the stalks of your

mushrooms, which you have chopped fine, six ounces of bread-crumbs, which you have soaked in consommé (Art. 1) and then pressed until nearly dry, a pinch of salt, pepper, and nutmeg, and four tablespoonfuls of tomato sauce. Mix all well together, and boil ten minutes. Then fill your mushrooms with the above mixture, sprinkle some bread-crumbs, and put a little melted butter on top. Send them to a gentle oven, until colored a light brown, and serve on toast, or with a Spanish sauce (Art. 80), to which add a glass of sherry, or with an Italian sauce (Art. 93), or a tomato sauce (Art. 90).

407. **Squash.** Peel and wash a squash, open it and take out the seeds, put it in a saucepan, with two quarts of water and a pinch of salt. When boiled tender, allow it to drain fifteen minutes, press it through a sieve, put it in a saucepan with four ounces of butter, a pinch of salt, and a little nutmeg, and serve very hot.

408. **Carrots Sautés au Beurre.** Scrape and wash some very young carrots, and boil them with a little salt, either whole or cut in pieces. When very tender, drain them, and put them in a saucepan, with some butter, a pinch of salt, and a tablespoonful of chopped parsley. Serve very hot. You may also serve them boiled, with a sauce béchamel (Art. 83).

409. **Chiccory with Cream.** Wash some chiccory, and boil for thirty minutes in three quarts of water, with a little salt. Then put in cold water for a moment, drain, and press the moisture from it. Chop it very fine. Put in a saucepan two ounces of butter, a tablespoonful of flour, a pinch of salt, pepper, and nutmeg; mix all well together, and add a glass of cream, and the same of consommé (Art. 1). Stir with a spoon on the fire until beginning to boil, then add your chiccory, and boil ten minutes. Mix with the yolks of three eggs a tablespoonful of cream, remove your saucepan from the fire, stir in your eggs, and serve. Place on top of the chiccory two hard-boiled eggs cut in quarters.

410. **Cabbage Sauté au Beurre.** Wash a cabbage, of about two pounds, boil it in two quarts of water, with a little salt, for about an hour. Put it for a moment in cold water, drain it, press out all the moisture, chop it, not too fine, and put it in a saucepan, with four ounces of butter, a pinch of salt and pepper, and serve very hot.

411. **Cabbage au Gratin.** Wash a cabbage, of about three pounds, boil it in boiling water about twenty minutes, then put it in cold water for a moment. Drain it, carefully press out all moisture, and place it in a saucepan, with half a pint of consommé (stock, [Art. 1](#)), four ounces of butter, a little salt, pepper, and nutmeg. Boil two hours. Place it in a deep dish, cover it with a sauce Allemande ([Art. 81](#)). Sprinkle bread-crumbs and grated cheese on top, and send to the oven until colored a nice brown.

412. **Cabbage farcied.** Wash a cabbage, of about three pounds, put it in boiling water and boil for half an hour, then plunge it in cold water for a moment. Chop fine a pound and a half of fresh pork, season with salt, pepper, nutmeg, and a little thyme. Remove the leaves from the center of your cabbage, and fill it with the above ingredients. Tie a buttered paper around the cabbage, and place a slice of thin pork on top. Then put your cabbage in a saucepan, filling it half the height of the cabbage with consommé (stock, [Art. 1](#)). Send it to the oven for about two hours, basting frequently with the consommé. Remove this buttered paper and pork, and serve around it a Spanish sauce ([Art. 80](#)), to which you have added the juice of a lemon.

413. **Brussels Sprouts.** Scrape and wash well two quarts of Brussels sprouts, put them in three quarts of boiling water, with half an ounce of salt. Boil rapidly until perfectly tender, drain them, and put them in a saucepan, with four ounces of butter. Mix well together, and, when very hot, serve instantly.

414. **Stewed Corn with Cream.** Boil ten ears of corn, then cut the corn from the cob, and put it in a saucepan, with two ounces of butter, a pinch of salt, and two glasses of cream. Boil gently ten minutes, and serve.

415. **New Orleans Corn Pudding.** Grate six ears of raw corn, which mix with a pint of milk and four eggs well beaten, add a little salt and white pepper, and send to the oven until colored a light brown on top.

416. **Macédoine of Vegetables.** Cut two ounces of carrots (with a vegetable-cutter or with a knife) in small pieces, and two ounces of turnips cut in the same manner, boil them until tender, and drain them. Also boil the same quantity of string-beans, cut in small pieces, and an equal portion of asparagus ends, and the tops of cauliflowers and green peas, which, when

boiled very tender, drain. Take half a pint of Spanish sauce, boil it a few minutes, with a pinch of sugar and nutmeg, add your vegetables, boil five minutes, and serve. Instead of Spanish sauce, you may also add your vegetables to a sauce Allemande (Art. 81), with a pinch of sugar and nutmeg. Heat your sauce until very hot, but do not allow it to boil. The vegetables for the above must all be boiled separately, as, in the same length of time, all will not be equally cooked. If you desire to avoid the trouble of preparing these vegetables yourself, they may be procured at any grocer's, canned or in bottles.

417. **Sourcrout.** Wash a quart of sourcrout, which drain, and put in a saucepan, with half a pound of bacon, a good pinch of pepper, and moisten with sufficient stock (from which the grease has not been removed) to cover it. Boil gently an hour and a half, add eight small sausages, which place in the middle of your sourcrout, boil thirty minutes, remove your bacon and sausages, drain the sourcrout, which arrange on a dish, placing the sausages around it, and also the bacon, cut in small pieces. You may serve with this dish, if desired, a dish of mashed potatoes.

418. **Lima Beans.** Boil three pints of Lima beans in plenty of water, and a little salt, until quite tender. Drain them and put them in a saucepan on the fire, with two ounces of butter, a pinch of salt, pepper, and nutmeg. Mix two yolks of eggs in a tablespoonful of water and the juice of a lemon, add them to your beans, with a tablespoonful of chopped parsley, and serve.

419. **Succotash.** Take a pint and a half of boiled Lima beans, and the same of boiled corn, cut from the cob. Mix them together in a saucepan on the fire, with six ounces of butter, half a glass of milk, a pinch of salt, pepper, and nutmeg, and serve very hot.

420. **Dried Lima Beans.** Soak three pints of Lima beans in water for twelve hours, and proceed as for fresh Lima beans (Art. 418).

421. **Mashed Potatoes.** Peel and wash eight medium-sized potatoes, cut them in pieces, and put them in a saucepan with a quart of cold water and a little salt. Boil until perfectly tender, drain, press through a sieve, and put them in a saucepan, with a pinch of salt and a glass of milk, and serve hot.

422. **Baked Mashed Potatoes.** Prepare your potatoes as the above, with the exception of the milk, place them in a pan in the oven, with some melted butter on top, and, when well browned, serve.

423. **Potato Croquettes.** Boil four potatoes, drain them, press them through a sieve, and then put them in a saucepan with an ounce of butter, a pinch of salt, pepper, nutmeg, and sugar. Heat them well, and add an egg. Let your mixture become very cold, form it into croquettes. Beat up three eggs, into which dip each croquette, and cover entirely with egg, then roll them in bread-crumbs, and fry in hot lard. When colored a light brown, drain them, and serve very hot.

424. **Mashed Potatoes with Bacon.** Cut a quarter of a pound of bacon in small pieces, also an onion, put them in a saucepan on the fire, and, when the onion begins to color, add a pint of water, several branches of parsley, inclosing two cloves, a branch of thyme, two bay-leaves, and tie all together; add eight potatoes, which you have washed, peeled, and cut in quarters, a pinch of pepper and nutmeg. When the potatoes are thoroughly cooked, remove your parsley with its seasoning, mash the potatoes well in the saucepan, and serve.

425. **Potatoes à l'Anglaise.** Wash eight potatoes, and boil them in cold water, with a pinch of salt. When thoroughly done, peel them, cut them in thin round slices, put them, with three ounces of butter, a pinch of salt, pepper, and nutmeg, in a saucepan on the fire, and, when very hot, serve.

426. **Potatoes à la Maître d'Hôtel.** Prepare your potatoes as the above. Just before serving add the juice of a lemon and a tablespoonful of chopped parsley. Another manner of preparing them: Proceed as for the foregoing, with the addition of half a glass of cream.

427. **Potatoes Sautés.** Prepare as the foregoing; then put them in a saucepan on the fire, with four ounces of melted butter and a pinch of salt; toss them in the pan until they are a good color, and serve them with a little chopped parsley on top.

428. **Potatoes à la Lyonnaise.** Boil your potatoes, and, when cold, cut them in round slices of medium thickness; cut two onions in slices, and put them with four ounces of butter in a frying-pan; when your onions are

colored very slightly, add your potatoes, toss them in the pan until they are a good color, drain them, and serve them with chopped parsley sprinkled over them.

429. **Potatoes à la Provençale.** Boil your potatoes, and, when cold, cut them in quarters; put in a saucepan on the fire for five minutes four tablespoonfuls of oil, a pinch of green onion, and quarter of the rind of a lemon chopped fine; then mix with your ingredients a tablespoonful of flour; add your potatoes, a little salt, pepper, nutmeg, and two ounces of butter; serve very hot, with some chopped parsley sprinkled on top.

430. **Hashed Potatoes with Cream.** Boil your potatoes, and, when cold, hash them fine, and put them in a saucepan with half a pint of cream, salt, pepper, a little nutmeg, and four ounces of butter; serve when very hot.

431. **Baked Hashed Potatoes.** Prepare as the foregoing; then put them in a dish about an inch and a half deep, level the potatoes on top with the blade of a knife, put a little melted butter on top, and send to the oven until nicely browned.

432. **Potatoes à l'Anna.** Cut up some raw potatoes very fine, put them in cold water for six hours, then drain them, season with salt and plenty of pepper; put them in a well-buttered pan, sprinkle bread-crumbs on top, and enough melted butter to cover them; send them to a very hot oven for about thirty-five minutes, or until they are well browned. Just before serving, drain off the butter, and put them on a dish.

433. **Fried Potatoes.** Peel eight medium-sized potatoes, cut them in slices, not too thick; wash them, then dry them on a napkin, fry them in plenty of hot lard on a quick fire, and, when a light brown, drain them, sprinkle them with salt, and serve.

434. **Fried Potatoes en Julienne.** Prepare and cook them as the above, and cut them in long, thin strips.

435. **Saratoga Potatoes.** Peel a pint of rather small potatoes, wash them in cold water, dry them on a napkin, and cut them in as thin slices as possible; then put half of your potatoes in a liberal quantity of very hot lard, taking care that they do not stick to each other. Fry them on a very quick fire, and, when a light brown and very crisp, drain them, and fry the

remaining half. Sprinkle a little salt on top, and serve them on a very hot dish.

436. **Potatoes à la Hollandaise.** Peel and wash fifteen medium-sized long potatoes, put them in cold water with a little salt, boil them, and, when well done, put them in a saucepan on the fire with two ounces of melted butter, remove them to the back of the range so as not to boil, shake them in the saucepan from time to time, and, when they have absorbed the butter, serve them in a very hot dish, and pour over them a sauce Hollandaise ([Art. 85](#)).

437. **Potatoes farcied.** Wash ten medium-sized potatoes—long potatoes, if you have them. Bake them, and cut the tops off with a sharp knife, and with a teaspoon scoop out the inside of each potato, which put in a bowl with two ounces of butter and the yolks of two eggs, a pinch of salt, pepper, and sugar. Fill the skins of your potatoes with this mixture, cover them with their tops, heat them well in the oven, and serve them very hot on a napkin. You may also prepare them with half potato and the other half chopped meat; finish the same, taking care to serve very hot.

438. **Potatoes à la Parisienne.** Peel and wash ten potatoes, scoop them out in little round balls with a potato-cutter for the purpose, which may be procured at any hardware-shop. Boil them five minutes, then put them in a frying-pan on the fire, with four ounces of melted butter, stir them in the pan, so that every potato shall be covered with butter, and send them to the oven to color. Sprinkle some salt and a little chopped parsley over them, and serve.

439. **Potatoes à la Duchesse.** Peel eight potatoes, cut them in pieces, wash them, and put them in a saucepan, with a quart of water and a pinch of salt. When they are thoroughly boiled, drain them, and put the saucepan at the side of the fire for ten minutes. Then add to them two ounces of butter, two eggs, a pinch of salt, the same of sugar, and press through a sieve. Form this mixture into little oval loaves, flat on top, on which, with the point of a knife, make designs, according to your taste. Put a little melted butter on top, send to the oven, and, when colored a nice brown, serve.

440. **Potatoes à la Parmentière.** Peel some potatoes, and cut them in form of a cork about three inches long, put them in a saucepan on the fire,

with enough Spanish sauce (Art. 80) to cover them, a pinch of salt, pepper, and sugar, and a glass of sherry. Simmer gently until the potatoes are perfectly tender, strain your sauce, pour it over your potatoes, and serve.

441. **Ragoût of Potatoes à la Paysanne.** Cut a bunch of chiccory in two through the middle, which boil fifteen minutes, put in cold water for a moment, drain, and press out all moisture. Peel ten potatoes, place them in a saucepan, with enough consommé (stock, Art. 1) to cover them, add your chiccory, three leeks cut in slices, a little salt, and season highly with pepper. Boil gently until your potatoes are nearly done, then add a little chopped chervil, and boil ten minutes longer. Your potatoes should be soft, without breaking. Serve very hot.

442. **Purée of French Chestnuts.** Remove the shells from two pounds of French chestnuts, put them in a frying-pan on the fire, with an ounce and a half of lard. Turn them over in the pan every now and then, and when you see that the species of skin which covers them is softened, and may be removed without difficulty, take them off the fire, for the purpose of doing so. Then put them in a saucepan, with a quart of consommé (stock, Art. 1), and, when the chestnuts are perfectly soft, drain them, press them through a sieve, heat them again with four ounces of butter, a pinch of salt and sugar, and serve.

443. **Purée of Artichokes.** Take the under part of ten artichokes, from which all leaves have been removed. Boil them in water and a little salt, drain them, and put them in a saucepan with a tablespoonful of flour, a pinch of salt, pepper, and nutmeg, and a glass and a half of consommé (stock, Art. 1 ). Boil twenty minutes, press through a sieve. Heat again on the fire, and serve as a vegetable, or garnish to meat or poultry.

444. **Purée of Jerusalem Artichokes.** Scrape and wash fifteen Jerusalem artichokes, boil them until tender in a pint of consommé (stock, Art. 1). Drain them, press them through a sieve, put them in a saucepan, with two ounces of butter, a pinch of salt and pepper, and, when hot, serve.

445. **Jerusalem Artichokes au Gratin.** Prepare and cook some artichokes exactly as for cauliflower au gratin (Art. 363).

446. **Purée of Green Peas.** Wash a quart of green peas, which put in a saucepan on the fire, with three pints of water, very little salt and pepper, half an ounce of ham, an onion cut in slices, and boil until soft. Then press them through a sieve, heat them again on the fire, adding four ounces of butter, a pinch of sugar, and serve.

www.ingramcontent.com/pod-product-compliance
Lightning Source LLC
Chambersburg PA
CBHW081623100526
44590CB00021B/3574